GRANT PARK

GRANT PARK

The Democratization
of Presidential Elections
1968–2008

CANDICE J. NELSON

BROOKINGS INSTITUTION PRESS
Washington, D.C.

Copyright © 2011
THE BROOKINGS INSTITUTION
1775 Massachusetts Avenue, N.W., Washington, DC 20036.
www.brookings.edu

Library of Congress Cataloging-in-Publication data

Nelson, Candice J., 1949–
    Grant Park : the democratization of presidential elections, 1968–2008 /
Candice J. Nelson.
        p. cm.
    Includes bibliographical references and index.
    Summary: "Takes a look at American presidential elections from 1968 to
2008—a period of great change in American society in general—and explains
how changes in technology, finance laws, party rules, political institutions, and
the electorate itself have affected the selection process and might again in the
upcoming election"—Provided by publisher.
    ISBN 978-0-8157-2184-0 (pbk. : alk. paper)
    1. Presidents—United States—Election—History—20th century.
2. Presidents—United States—Election—History—21st century. I. Title.
JK524.N45 2011
    324.973'092—dc23   2011036942

9 8 7 6 5 4 3 2 1

Printed on acid-free paper

Typeset in Sabon

Composition by Cynthia Stock
Silver Spring, Maryland

Printed by R. R. Donnelley
Harrisonburg, Virginia

For my granddaughter
Elina Kaede

CONTENTS

ACKNOWLEDGMENTS

THIS BOOK WOULD NOT have been possible without the support of a number of people. Most particularly, I thank my colleague and mentor at American University, Distinguished Professor James A. Thurber, for his encouragement and support; and American University School of Public Affairs Dean William LeoGrande. My graduate assistants, Alyssa Mowitz and Jon Weakley, provided invaluable research support. At the Brookings Institution Press, I would like to thank Christopher Kelaher, marketing director and senior acquisitions editor; former acquisitions editor Mary Kwak; Janet Walker, managing editor; Susan Woollen for the cover design; and Diane Hammond, who edited the manuscript. I also thank the anonymous reviewers: the book is better for their comments and suggestions.

INTRODUCTION

IN THE FORTY YEARS between the 1968 and 2008 presidential elections the United States changed as a country and so did the way in which presidents are elected. The presidential election process became much more democratic over those years. In 1968 the nomination process was dominated by backroom politics; by 2008 the nomination process was one in which millions of people could vote for nominees through primaries and caucuses. In 1968 both major party nominees were white men; in 2008 an African American was the Democratic Party's presidential nominee, and a woman was the Republican Party's vice presidential nominee. In 1968 elections were funded by large, undisclosed donations; by 2008 both large and small donations were fully disclosed. In 1968 there were no presidential debates during the general election; by 2008 both presidential and vice presidential debates were an established part of the fall campaigns.

The election process also changed during the forty-year period. Election reforms made it easier for Americans to register to vote. Technological advances enabled campaign workers to more easily communicate among themselves and with potential voters, and supporters could more easily communicate with the campaigns. The American electorate itself became more diverse, with more women, young people, and minorities participating in the electoral process.

This book examines the democratization of the presidential election process through the metaphor of Grant Park. During the Democratic Convention in 1968, Chicago's Grant Park was the site of rioting (largely instigated by police action) by young people, many of whom were African Americans, shut out of the nomination process. Forty years later thousands of Americans, many young and many African American, gathered in Grant Park in the early morning hours of November 3, 2008, to celebrate the election of the first African American president.

1968

Nineteen sixty-eight had been a tumultuous year for the Democratic Party. On March 31, two weeks after Senator Eugene McCarthy of Minnesota had won 42 percent of the vote in the New Hampshire primary, President Lyndon Johnson announced that he would not be a candidate for reelection. McCarthy had run as a candidate opposed to U.S. involvement in the war then raging in Vietnam. Just a day after McCarthy came close to beating President Johnson in the New Hampshire primary, New York senator Robert Kennedy, brother of the late President John F. Kennedy, entered the primaries. Kennedy secured the nomination after winning the California primary June 5, only to be struck down by an assassin's bullet later that night. Hubert Humphrey, President Johnson's vice president, then became the de facto nominee. Yet Humphrey had competed in no primaries or caucuses in 1968.

Humphrey's likely nomination, despite strong showings in the primaries by antiwar candidates McCarthy and Kennedy, caused considerable unrest among those opposing the Vietnam War. Antiwar sentiment had been rampant during the Democratic primary, and the frustration of the antiwar community boiled over outside the Democratic Convention, held at the International Amphitheater in downtown Chicago. The antiwar views were largely ignored by delegates inside the convention hall, but anger at the Democratic Party and its nominee raged outside the convention, as antiwar activists demonstrated in Grant Park. The images were stark: the delegates to the Democratic Convention, mostly white, middle-aged men, nominating a candidate who had not competed in the nomination process, while young people demonstrating against the war and the party's nominee were being teargassed, maced, and beaten in Grant Park and other areas of the city.

2008

Forty years and just over three months later, Grant Park was again the focus of attention. This time, however, those shut out of the convention in 1968 were a big part of the tens of thousands celebrating the election of the first African American president in the history of the United States. Grant Park was not the scene of anger, frustration, and bitterness it had been in the summer of 1968 but rather a scene of celebration, hope, and inclusiveness. When President-elect Obama addressed the more than 125,000 people in the park just after midnight on election night, he looked out at a sea of faces—many of them similar to those who had been shut out of the nomination process forty years earlier.

This volume chronicles how the presidential election process and its three parts—the nomination, convention, and general election—changed between 1968 and 2008 and anticipates what the process might look like in 2012. The presidential route in 2008 was nothing like that in 1968, nor was it like those in 1976, or 1984, or 1992. The role of the nominating convention evolved (or, more accurately, devolved) between 1968 and 2008. The general election process, while still governed by the Electoral College, also changed in the forty-year interim.

BETWEEN 1968 AND 2008

Following the 1968 convention the Democratic Party established a series of commissions that profoundly changed the way candidates were nominated. Hubert Humphrey had won the nomination in 1968 because the nomination process was largely controlled by state caucuses and conventions that allowed party insiders to control state delegations to the convention. Beginning in 1972 the nomination process gradually evolved from a convention-dominated one to one in which the majority of delegates are chosen in state primaries. Once the primary became the main vehicle for nominating delegates, the primary process itself changed, with more and more states electing to hold their primaries closer and closer to the start of the formal nomination process.

Parallel to changes in the nominating process were changes in the financing of presidential elections. The Federal Election Campaign Act of 1971 (FECA) provided for voluntary, full public funding of the general election, and partial public funding of the nomination process, beginning with the 1976 presidential election. For a while the changes in the nomination process and the opportunity to receive partial public funding worked in tandem, allowing lesser known candidates to either win the nomination (Jimmy Carter in 1976) or compete strongly for the nomination (Gary Hart in 1984). However, in 1992 the campaign funding process began to crumble with the influx of so-called soft money, and by 2008 the process that worked so well when it was first enacted was in shambles, with none of the first-tier candidates in either party accepting partial public funds during the nomination process, and one of the major party candidates—Barack Obama—rejecting public funds in the general election, the first time a major party nominee had done so since the enactment of FECA.

The role of the nominating conventions also changed. While still the formal mechanism for nominating the Democratic and Republican candidates for president, the evolving shifts in the nomination process meant that by 1988 the actual candidates for president were known well before the conventions took place. Even in 2008, with wide-open fields for both the Democratic and Republican nominations and the longest quest for the nomination since 1984 for the Democrats, both Barack Obama and John McCain had enough delegates to claim their respective party nominations three months before the conventions. The inevitability of the major party nominees led to a spiraling downward dance between the political parties and the broadcast media, where the media covered less and less of the conventions and the parties tried to make what was covered a way to connect to the electorate in the fall campaign. By 2008 the major broadcast and cable networks devoted only one hour of prime-time coverage to the conventions, so the parties had to fit into one hour each night what they had previously presented in three or four hours.

The years between 1968 and 2008 also saw changes in the general election. There was a gradual winnowing of states in which candidates seriously competed. States became labeled as red states (states strongly favoring Republican candidates), blue states (states strongly favoring Democratic candidates), and, eventually, purple states (states moving from red to blue or blue to red). Candidates competed in a dozen to two dozen so-called battleground states, which meant that some states, including those with the largest populations (California and New York, blue states, and Texas, a red state), saw virtually no campaign activity.

Presidential debates also once again became part of the general election. After the famous Nixon-Kennedy debates in 1960 no presidential candidates debated until 1976. Presidential debates gradually returned in

1976 and 1980, sponsored by the League of Women Voters. In 1987, in a move to institutionalize the debates, the Commission on Presidential Debates was created, and the commission has sponsored the debates since 1988. Debates are now expected between both the presidential and vice presidential candidates. While there is disagreement as to how important the debates are to the outcome of the election, they are watched by millions of Americans during each general election, and numerous memorable moments have come out of the debates in the last three decades.

PLAN OF THE BOOK

The first four chapters of the book examine the changes in the presidential election process between 1968 and 2008. Chapter 1 examines the presidential campaign finance system. From 1976 until 1988 the system worked much as the drafters of the Federal Election Campaign Act of 1971 hoped it would. One goal of the FECA was to eliminate the opportunity for wealthy contributors to contribute large amounts of money with little if any disclosure. Beginning in 1976 wealthy interests, be they individual or group, had much less opportunity to influence the nomination and general elections. Also, with its provisions for partial public funding, lesser known candidates had an opportunity to compete with better known candidates for the nomination. By 1992, however, large campaign contributions had crept back into the presidential election process in the form of soft money. By 2000 public funding of presidential elections began to erode when Republican candidate George W. Bush announced he would decline partial public funding in the nomination period.

Chapter 2 looks at changes in the presidential nomination process. The evolution of the process from a convention and caucus system in 1968 to a mainly primary system in 2008 is examined. The chapter also looks at the gradual change from a nomination process spread over three months to one in which the front-loading of primaries and caucuses meant that a candidate could lock up the party nomination early—in February or March. Differences between the Democratic and Republican nomination processes are also covered: delegates to the Democratic Convention are assigned proportionally within states, while the Republican Party allows a winner-take-all system, in which the candidate who wins a plurality of the votes in a state collects all of the state's delegates. The differences in the two systems have important consequences for the outcomes of the nomination process.

This chapter also looks at the prenomination process. As the nomination process became increasingly front-loaded and the campaign finance process began to erode, candidates began to plan for the nomination earlier and earlier, both organizationally and financially. Candidate George W. Bush's fundraising prowess in early 1999 drove almost all of his competitors out of the race that summer, before any votes were cast. Several candidates' quests for their party's 2008 nomination were well under way before the 2006 congressional elections had ended. Potential Republican candidates in 2012 began hiring staff in 2009, over three years before the election.

Chapter 3 looks at the changes in the role of the nominating conventions. Between 1968 and 2008 the role of conventions changed from being the culmination of the nomination process, when the actual nominees were decided, to being the kickoff of the general election. As media network coverage of the conventions dwindled from gavel-to-gavel coverage to just an hour of prime time coverage, the candidates and the parties had to rethink how best to present their messages not only to convention delegates but also to the general election audience.

Chapter 4 examines the general election process—the evolution of battleground states, the role of the debates, and the contentious and drawn-out battle in 2000. Between 1968 and 2008 the candidates moved from campaigning in all fifty states, as Richard Nixon famously claimed he would do in 1960, to campaigning only in so-called battleground states. Even before the Republican candidate was chosen in 1988, the Republican Party had decided that its candidate would campaign in only twenty-five states—the other twenty-five would receive no resources, no visits, no attention at all. This winnowing of states continued through 2008 and will continue through 2012. The states the Republican and Democratic candidates identify as battleground were remarkably similar in the 1990s and 2000 and 2004, though Barack Obama expanded the states in this category in 2008. This chapter also looks at the role of presidential debates, as discussed above, in the general election process. Finally, the chapter looks at the 2000 election, when five weeks transpired between Election Day and the day the new president was finally known.

Chapters 5 through 7 look at broader changes in the United States that affected presidential elections. Chapter 5 looks at the increasingly important role of technology in presidential campaigns. The technology available to campaigns in 2008 was unheard of in 1968. The changes between 2000 and 2004, and again between 2004 and 2008, affected the way campaigns were able to interact both internally with their organizations and externally with potential supporters. The Internet allowed campaign organizations to communicate much faster and less expensively and to reach volunteers, contributors, and potential voters through not only traditional campaign techniques but also new social media such as blogs, Twitter, and Facebook.

Chapter 6 looks at changes in voting rules over the past two decades. Voting in presidential elections no longer occurs on just one Election Day. Registration and voting rules have been changed to allow absentee voting and, more important for turnout, no-excuse absentee voting, early in-person voting, and in some states, Election Day registration and voting. Registration no longer occurs just in election offices but can also be done at departments of motor vehicles and other state agencies. This chapter examines how changes in voting rules affect presidential election strategies, particularly in the most recent elections.

Chapter 7 looks at trends in voter engagement and the consequences of changing U.S. demographics. Following the 2010 census the United States saw increases in minority groups, particularly Latinos. These changes have implications for the presidential election in 2012, as both the Democratic and Republican parties court this increasingly important demographic group. Latinos will be particularly important in southwestern states and could change the calculation as to which states are considered battleground states. The 2004 and 2008 elections saw increased engagement by young people ages eighteen to twenty-nine, a traditionally low-turnout demographic group.

Chapter 8 looks forward to the 2012 election, studying the state of presidential elections going into the 2012 election cycle. Both the Republican and Democratic parties established commissions to examine the nomination process, and the recommendations of those commissions changed the rules for the nomination process in 2012. Public funding of presidential elections, a process all but obliterated in 2008, will likely be extinct in 2012, and the bar for fundraising will be the one set by the Obama campaign in 2008. The 2010 census changed the Electoral College map, as some states picked up Electoral College votes and others lost them. This chapter examines how these factors might affect the 2012 presidential election.

Finally, chapter 9 draws some conclusions about the democratization of presidential elections in the forty-year span between the demonstrations in Grant Park in 1968 and the celebration forty years later. The chapter also looks at the democratization of presidential elections since the 2008 election.

CHAPTER ONE

CAMPAIGN FINANCE

THE PASSAGE OF THE Federal Election Campaign Act of 1971 began a process that fundamentally reformed the way presidential campaigns in the United States are financed. Beginning with the 1976 election, presidential candidates were, for the first time, eligible for partial public funding of their nomination campaign and full public funding of their general election. Public funding enabled candidates who did not have personal wealth, access to wealthy contributors, or high name recognition to compete for the presidency. This chapter examines the campaign finance process between 1976 and 2008, the costs of presidential campaigns during that period, and how the changes in campaign finance between 2000 and 2008 affected those costs.

THE CAMPAIGN FINANCE PROCESS

The Tillman Act, passed in 1907, prohibited corporate contributions in federal elections, and the Taft-Hartley Act, passed in 1947, extended the prohibition to contributions from labor unions. The Federal Corrupt Practices Act, requiring House and Senate candidates to disclose contributions and expenditures, was passed in 1925, but it was not strictly enforced and was not particularly effective in regulating campaign finance in federal elections. When President Kennedy was elected in 1960 he expressed interest in reforming the campaign finance system, but his assassination in 1963 interrupted those efforts. Legislation to reform the campaign finance system was considered in Congress during the 1960s,

9

but no law was enacted. It was not until the early 1970s that major legislation to replace the Federal Corrupt Practices Act was passed.[1]

In late 1971 and early 1972 two pieces of campaign finance legislation were enacted into law—the Federal Election Campaign Act of 1971 (FECA) and the Revenue Act of 1971. The FECA required greater disclosure of campaign contributions, including requiring political parties and candidates for federal office to report both total expenditures and the names, addresses, and occupations of contributors. The act also established regular disclosure reports of contributions and expenditures. The Revenue Act of 1971 established the Presidential Election Campaign Fund, which was to be funded by voluntary tax checkoffs, with the expectation that public funding of presidential campaigns would follow.[2]

The disclosure requirements of the FECA of 1971 shed new light on the funding of presidential elections. Both President Nixon's 1972 reelection campaign, the Committee to Re-Elect the President (CREEP), and Senator McGovern's campaign benefited from the largesse of wealthy contributors, with some contributors to the Nixon campaign giving as much as $2 million to the campaign.[3] The Watergate investigation that examined the practices of CREEP also found numerous instances of illegal corporate contributions.[4]

CAMPAIGN FINANCE RULES

The Watergate revelations led to calls for new campaign finance regulations. The 1974 amendments to the FECA established the campaign finance rules that largely exist today. The amendments established contribution limits for individuals, political parties, and political action committees (PACs). The amendments also established voluntary public funding of the presidential general election, partial public funding of the nomination process, and public funds for the presidential nominating conventions. Limits were set on the amount of money that could be spent on the nomination and in the general elections by candidates accepting public funding. The nomination limit was $10 million and the general election limit was $20 million, both indexed for inflation. Finally, the amendments created a new federal agency, the Federal Election Commission, to administer the FECA.[5]

The 1976 election was the first presidential election under the new campaign finance system. The regulations that governed the presidential campaign process during the 1976 elections continue today. First, candidates choose whether or not to accept partial public funding during the nomination process and then whether or not to accept full public funding in the general election. Candidates are not required to accept partial public funding during the primary process or full public funding in the general election, and agreeing to public funding for one election period does not commit candidates to public funding for the other.

To qualify for partial public funding during the nomination process candidates have to raise $5,000 in each of twenty states in amounts of $250 or less from individuals. Once a candidate qualifies for partial public funding, he or she receives matching funds from the federal treasury. For every $250 raised from individuals, a candidate receives $250 in funds. Candidates accepting partial public funding must also accept both state-by-state spending limits and an overall spending limit for the nomination period. State-by-state spending limits are determined by a formula based on the state's population. The overall primary spending limit is 50 percent of the general election spending limit. To continue to qualify for matching funds during the nomination period candidates must receive at least 10 percent of the vote in two consecutive primaries or caucuses.

During the general election the Democratic and Republican candidates—the major party candidates—qualify for full public funding once they are certified at the party's national nominating conventions as their parties' nominees. Third-party candidates qualify for some public funding in the general election only if their party's candidate received 5 percent or more of the popular vote in the previous presidential general election. First-time third-party candidates whose party did not exist in the previous election receive public funding only after the election, making public funding essentially useless to them during the election itself.

THE EARLY YEARS OF THE NEW RULES

While the campaign finance process on its face seems fairly straightforward, it took only a few election cycles for problems to surface. First, at the time the 1974 amendments to the FECA were passed, the threshold for qualifying for public funds was seen as a financial hurdle sufficient to weed out third-party candidates and marginal candidates unlikely to receive their party's nomination. However, less than a decade later third-party candidates began to qualify for federal funds. Sonia Johnson, a candidate of the Citizens Party, received matching funds in the 1984 presidential election. Lyndon LaRouche, a perennial candidate for president, also qualified for federal funds in the 1984 election. In 1992 John Hagelin, the candidate of the Natural Law Party, and Lenora Fulani, the New Alliance Party candidate, both received federal funds. Even major party candidates with little chance of receiving their party's nomination were able to qualify for federal funds. For example, in 2008 Democrats Mike Gravel and Dennis Kucinich both received federal matching funds—Gravel about $215,000 and Kucinich slightly over $1 million; Republican candidates Duncan Hunter and Tom Tancredo also received matching funds, Hunter $453,000 and Tancredo about $2.2 million. Ralph Nader, running as an independent in 2008, received almost $900,000 in federal matching funds.[6]

A second problem that quickly arose was the state-by-state spending limits. These limits are determined by the state's population but do not take into account the state's importance in the nomination process. For example, the earliest primary and caucus states, New Hampshire and Iowa, had relatively low spending limits in 2008—$841,000 and $1.5 million, respectively, despite their prominence in the nomination process. California, on the other hand, a state that in recent years has played a minor role in the nomination process, had a spending limit in 2008 of just over $18 million.[7]

Despite these unanticipated consequences of the 1974 amendments, the new campaign process worked as legislators had hoped when drafting the legislation. Wealthy donors were removed from the campaign finance process, there was transparency in contributions and expenditures, and lesser known candidates were able to compete on a relatively even playing field with better known candidates. Primary matching funds, coupled with reforms in the nomination process, allowed lesser known candidates to slowly become known to voters over the course of the nomination period. For example, Jimmy Carter was a relatively unknown Georgia governor when he finished second to "undecided" in the Iowa caucuses in 1976. While not a well-funded candidate initially, his primary and caucus successes led to campaign contributions, and the contributions, matched by public funds, enabled Carter to build a campaign organization, gain name recognition and support among the Democratic primary electorate, and eventually secure his party's nomination.

The former Colorado Democratic senator Gary Hart is an even better example of the confluence of the campaign finance process and the nomination process in the 1970s and 1980s. Walter Mondale, who had been vice president during Jimmy Carter's presidency, was widely seen as the likely Democratic presidential nominee in 1984. However, when Gary Hart finished second to Mondale in the Iowa caucuses and then went on to win the New Hampshire primary, Hart, virtually unknown before the Iowa caucuses, saw money pour into his campaign. Because of matching funds and a nomination process that extended from February until June, Hart was able to compete financially against the better funded Mondale campaign through the final primaries in California and New Jersey in early June. While Mondale eventually secured the nomination, federal matching funds allowed Hart, a little-known candidate at the start of the primary season, to compete with the party's front-runner for the nomination.

The Breakdown of the Campaign Finance Process

The symbiotic relationship between the nomination and campaign finance processes began to break down with the front-loading of the nomination process. As there became less time between primaries, lesser known candidates had less time to use matching funds to develop name recognition and support among voters. For example, in 1988 Michael Dukakis, the eventual Democratic nominee, won the New Hampshire primary and then a series of state contests on March 8, the first Super Tuesday. As the field rapidly narrowed, other lesser known candidates seeking the Democratic nomination that year, such as the former Arizona governor Bruce Babbitt, had only weeks (rather than months) to use matching funds to introduce themselves to Democratic primary voters. In 1992 Bill Clinton essentially wrapped up the Democratic nomination in early March, leaving other matching-fund recipients that year—Bob Kerrey, Tom Harkin, Paul Tsongas, and Jerry Brown—unable to extend their campaigns into the spring.

In 1996 the presidential campaign finance system itself began to break down. Steven Forbes, heir to the *Forbes* magazine dynasty, decided to seek the Republican Party's nomination but not to accept partial public funds in his run for the nomination. Before 1996 only one major party candidate had declined partial public funding. John Connolly, seeking the Republican Party's nomination in 1976, declined partial public funding.[8] Forbes ultimately lost the nomination to Senator Robert Dole but, in the process, forced Dole to spend the limit for the nomination process. As a result, when Dole became the presumptive nominee of the Republican Party in March, he was legally not allowed to spend money until August, when he became the official nominee. Meanwhile, President Bill Clinton, seeking reelection, had no primary opponent and thus had money to spend between the end of the primaries in April and the Democratic Convention in August.

To bridge the gap between when Dole secured the Republican nomination in March and when he became the official nominee of the party in August, the Republican Party ran a series of issue ads to support Dole's nomination. Issue ads first surfaced during the 1993 debate over President Clinton's health care proposals, but in 1996 the ads moved from a focus on policy to commercials for or against candidates for office. Because the Supreme Court, in *Buckley* v. *Valeo,* had ruled that political commercials that explicitly advocated for the support or defeat of a candidate, using the so-called magic words (*vote for, vote against, elect, defeat*), had to be paid for with hard money, political parties and interest groups were able to use soft money, described later in this chapter, to run ads that did not explicitly advocate for or against candidates. The Republican Party took advantage of this loophole in campaign finance law to counter ads that the Clinton campaign ran between March and August of 1996.

When Governor George W. Bush of Texas decided to seek the Republican Party's nomination in 2000, he learned from Dole's experience in 1996. To ensure that he had enough money to be competitive throughout the nomination period, Bush decided to opt out of partial public funding. His decision paid off; during the second quarter of 1999, six months before the primaries and caucuses would begin, it was rumored that Bush would report raising between $21 million and $23 million. In fact, he raised $35 million during the quarter, at that time the most money that any presidential candidate had ever raised in a single quarter. The primary spending limit for 2000 was $33.5 million.[9] Over the summer of 1999 most of Bush's opponents dropped out of the race for the Republican nomination, often citing their inability to compete with Bush's fundraising prowess.

Four years later Howard Dean, then the governor of Vermont, raised $14 million during the third quarter of 2003. That was the most money any Democratic candidate for the nomination had ever raised in one quarter. Emboldened by his fundraising success, Dean announced that he would forgo partial public funding during the upcoming nomination contest. Massachusetts Senator John Kerry, also seeking the Democratic nomination in 2004, believed that to be competitive with Dean he too would have to opt out of partial public funding during the nomination process. In December of 2003 Kerry took out a $6 million mortgage on his Beacon Hill home to rescue his primary campaign from the brink of bankruptcy. In the end, Dean raised $40 million, yet he was out of the primaries in February, after losing both the Iowa caucuses and the New Hampshire primary. Kerry, the eventual Democratic nominee, raised $234.6 million during the nomination period; President George W. Bush, seeking re-election, raised $269.9 million.[10] With both major party nominees opting out of the partial public funding process, the 2004 election, in effect, marked the end of partial public funding during the nomination period, and it was widely expected that no serious candidate for the presidency in 2008 would accept public funds during the nomination contest.

For the 2008 presidential election cycle the limit on spending during the nomination period for candidates who accepted partial public funds was $42.05 million. Given the amount spent by Bush and Kerry in 2004, almost all first-tier candidates decided to opt out of the public funding process. Only former Democratic vice presidential candidate John Edwards accepted matching funds, though several second-tier candidates—Senators Christopher Dodd and Joe Biden, Representative Dennis Kucinich, and the former Alaska senator Mike Gravel on the Democratic side and Republican Representatives Duncan Hunter and Tom Tancredo—did accept matching funds.

The final nail in the coffin for the public funding of presidential elections occurred during the general election. Then senator Barack Obama, because of his fundraising successes in 2007 and during the primaries in 2008, decided to opt out of full public funding during the general election. The 2008 election was the first time a major party candidate declined public funding in the general election, though Ross Perot, running on the Reform Party ticket in 1992, privately financed his campaign.[11] The general election spending limit for candidates who accepted public funding in 2008 was $84 million. Given that he raised $454 million during the nomination period, Obama was reasonably confident that he could raise more than $84 million for the general election. By opting out of public funding, he was unconstrained by the spending limit. In the end, Obama's calculations proved correct. He raised over $300 million during the general election, including a record $150 million in September alone. In total, Obama spent $745 million on his successful presidential bid, dwarfing both what Senator McCain was able to raise and spend and what other presidential candidates had done in the past. Reflecting on the presidential finance system after the election, McCain campaign manager Steve Schmidt said, "Public financing is over."[12] Schmidt estimated that the Republican Party nominee in 2012 would need to run "really close to a billion-dollar campaign" to be competitive with a likely Obama reelection campaign.

THE COSTS OF PRESIDENTIAL CAMPAIGNS

Before the passage of the Federal Election Campaign of 1971 it was difficult to obtain precise calculations of the amount of money spent on presidential campaigns, because there were essentially no enforceable disclosure requirements. Much of what is known about pre-FECA presidential expenditures comes from the research of the late political scientist Herbert Alexander and the data collected by the Citizens' Research Foundation. Alexander estimates that the amount spent in the 1968 Republican nomination and general election contests was $45 million: $20 million during the nomination process and $25 million in the general election. He estimates the amount spent in the Democratic nomination and general election contests was $37 million: $25 million during the nomination process and $12 million in the general election.[13] Regarding the 1972 presidential elections, Alexander estimates that $69 million was spent in the Republican contests, with almost all of that being spent in the general election as President Nixon faced no serious challenge to his nomination, and that $63 million was spent in the Democratic presidential contests, $33 million in the nomination process and $30 million in the general election.

The 1976 presidential election was the first election under public funding and the spending limits imposed on candidates accepting public funding. Table 1-1 lists the primary and general election spending

TABLE 1-1. Presidential Spending Limits, 1976–2008[a]
$Millions

Year	Primary	General
1976	10.9	21.8
1980	14.7	29.4
1984	20.2	40.4
1988	23.1	46.1
1992	27.6	55.2
1996	30.9	61.8
2000	33.7	67.5
2004	37.3	74.6
2008	42.0	84.1

Source: Federal Election Commission.
a. Candidates can spend an additional 20 percent of the limit on legal and accounting expenses.

limits for the years 1976 through 2008. The 1976 limits for both the nomination and general elections were well below what was spent in the 1972 elections. Between 1976 and 2008 the limits were adjusted upward, but slowly. With partial public funding for the nomination period and full public funding for the general election, the campaign finance system enabled candidates with limited wealth and name recognition to contest for their party's nomination and to run in the general election free of special interests. The system worked as long as all candidates seeking the nomination or running in the general election participated in the system. With the exception of John Connolly in 1976, all major party candidates had accepted partial public funding for the nomination process until 2000, and full public funding for the general election until 2008.

Table 1-2 lists presidential campaign spending in the 2000, 2004, and 2008 elections, elections in which candidates began to decline public funding. The Bush campaign in 2000 was the first primary campaign in which a major party candidate did not accept partial public funding and the limits that accompany such funding. As table 1-2 shows, the Bush primary campaign outspent that of the Democratic nominee, Al Gore, by more than two to one. The parity between nominees that had existed for more than three decades disappeared during the 2000 election, and by 2004 the slow growth in the costs of presidential elections also vanished.

TABLE 1-2. Presidential Spending by Party Nominees, 2000, 2004, 2008
$Millions

	Primary		General	
Year	Democrats	Republicans	Democrats	Republicans
2000[a]	42.47	89.15	67.6	67.6
2004[b]	224.79	268.86	74.62	74.62
2008[c]	376.5	177.8	369.2	84.1

a. John C. Green and Nathan S. Bigelow, "The 2000 Presidential Nominations: The Costs of Innovation," in *Financing the 2000 Election,* edited by David B. Magleby (Brookings, 2002), p. 55.

b. Federal Election Commission (www.fec.gov/press/press2005/20050203pressum/presdisb2004full.pdf).

c. Anthony Corrado, "Fundraising Strategies in the 2008 Presidential Campaign," in *Campaigns and Elections American Style,* edited by James A. Thurber and Candice J. Nelson, 3rd ed. (Westview, 2009), p. 112.

The rapid escalation in the costs of presidential elections between 1996 and 2000 was also exacerbated by the increase in the use of soft money by the two major political parties and by interest groups. When public funding of presidential campaigns began in 1976, candidates decided to use their public allocation for voter contact activities, which meant there was no money for traditional party-building activities, such as voter registration and get-out-the-vote drives. A series of Federal Election Commission advisory opinions in 1979 allowed political parties to raise soft money, so named because such funds are not subject to the hard and fast limits of campaign finance law but instead are used for party building. Because soft money was outside the limits of campaign finance laws, the amounts of money that parties could raise was unlimited, as were the sources of this money. Corporations and labor unions, forbidden from contributing hard dollars from their treasuries to political candidates, were allowed to contribute soft money to political parties. Between the 1996 and 2000 elections the amount of soft money raised by party campaign committees increased dramatically; Republican Party committees increased their soft money funds by 73 percent between 1996 and 2000; Democratic Party committees' soft money almost doubled in the four-year period and almost equaled their hard money receipts in 2000.[14] Much of the soft money raised by the parties was used for issue ads in support of or in opposition to political candidates, just as the Republican Party had done in support of Bob Dole's candidacy in 1996.

Campaign finance reform legislation had been percolating in Congress in various forms since the late 1980s, but passage had not been successful. However, following the 2000 election, the first campaign finance reform legislation since the 1970s was passed. The Bipartisan Campaign Finance Reform Act (BCRA)—often referred to as McCain-Feingold, after its two chief sponsors, Senators John McCain and Russ Feingold— went into effect following the 2002 midterm elections. The BCRA has two main provisions: it prohibits political parties from receiving soft money contributions, and it puts strict requirements on how issue ads can be funded. It also raises individual and party contribution limits and indexes contribution limits for inflation. As a result of the BCRA, the unlimited soft money contributions that had crept into presidential elections in the 1996 and 2000 elections were eliminated, as was the use of campaign advertising in the guise of issue advocacy.

Despite concerns that the Democratic Party, because of its disproportionate reliance on soft money in the 2000 presidential election, would be underfunded in 2004 as a consequence of the BCRA, the DNC actually slightly exceeded the RNC in the amount of money raised; the DNC raised $404 million in hard money and the RNC raised $393 million.[15] However, immediately following the enactment of the BCRA there was serious concern among progressive political actors that the Democratic nominee in 2004 would have difficulty matching the expenditures of the Republican Party, which had for decades been much more successful in raising hard money, and of the Bush reelection campaign. These Democrats used a new form of political activity, 527 organizations, to engage in the 2004 election. (These tax-exempt organizations are named after section 527 of the U.S. Internal Revenue Code.)

The 527 organizations that were created following the BCRA enabled wealthy individuals and interest groups to again play a role in presidential elections. These new organizations could not expressly advocate for a candidate nor could they coordinate with candidates or their campaigns, but they could raise and spend unlimited amounts of money, and they were not required to disclose their activities to the FEC. To counteract the expected fundraising prowess of the Republican Party and the Bush campaign, two new 527 organizations were formed to help the 2004 Democratic nominee. One, America Coming Together (ACT) would focus on grassroots organization and get-out-the-vote activities; the other, the Media Fund, would focus on communicating the Democratic message. During the 2004 presidential election ACT spent just over $78 million, and the Media Fund spent almost $54.5 million, making them two of the top three 527 organizations in spending during the 2004 election cycle.[16]

While there was more 527 activity in support of the Democratic Party and the Kerry campaign in 2004, there were also 527 organizations whose activities supported the Bush campaign. One of the most influential of these organizations was Swift Boat Veterans for Truth. SBVT was a 527 organization formed to criticize John Kerry's war record in Vietnam. SBVT ran its first television ad criticizing Kerry in early August, shortly after the conclusion of the Democratic Convention in Boston. The ad ran in only a few states, at a relatively small buy, but it received considerable play in the press.[17]

The Kerry campaign was slow to respond to the Swift Boat ads, in part because the ad buy itself was so small and restricted to only three states but also because of the funding for the general election in 2004. Both Kerry and Bush accepted public funding for their general election campaigns in 2004. They became eligible for that funding when they formally accepted their party's nomination and, once they accepted public funding, could accept no other funds. The problem the Kerry campaign faced was that the Democratic Convention was at the end of July; the Republican Convention wasn't until the end of August. That meant that Kerry's general election funds were spread over three months, while Bush's funds were spread over only two months. The Kerry campaign hoped to conserve its funds during the month of August, and responding to the Swift Boat ad when it first aired would have depleted those funds. SBVT ran two more ads in August, and Kerry finally responded to those ads in late August, but most political observers agreed that Kerry's response was too little, too late and contributed to his defeat in the general election.[18]

THE 2008 ELECTION

At the beginning of 2007, predictions were that to be competitive during the nomination process candidates would need to raise $100 million by the end of 2007. It was also assumed that Senator Hillary Clinton, the presumed front-runner for the Democratic nomination, and Senator John McCain, a front-runner for the Republican nomination, would be best able to raise those amounts, given Senator Clinton's fundraising successes in her two Senate elections and her access to her husband's fundraising network and Senator McCain's fundraising network from his 2000 presidential bid.

On April 1, 2007, the Clinton campaign announced that it had raised approximately $26 million during the first quarter of the year, putting the campaign on track to raise $100 million by the end of the year. Clinton seemingly had earned her reputation as front-runner, as least financially, outraising her closest competitor, John Edwards, by $12 million.[19] However, three days later the Obama campaign announced that it had raised $25 million in the first quarter, a staggering figure for a candidate's first foray onto the national stage.[20] Three months later the Obama campaign, by raising $32.8 million in the second quarter of 2007, exceeded the Clinton campaign's fundraising in that quarter: $26.5 million.[21] The Clinton and Obama campaigns continued to set fundraising records in 2007, with the Clinton campaign raising $23 million in both the third and fourth quarters of 2007 and the Obama campaign raising $19 million in the third quarter and $21 million in the fourth quarter.[22]

The McCain campaign was not so fortunate: it raised just under $13 million during the first quarter of 2007, less than both Mitt Romney ($20 million) and Rudy Giuliani ($14 million).[23] McCain's disappointing fundraising in the first quarter led to a revamping of his fundraising operation, but the figures for the second quarter, under a new fundraising scheme, were just as disappointing—McCain raised just over $11 million in the second quarter, once again trailing Romney ($13.8 million) and Giuliani ($17 million). The second-quarter fundraising numbers led to a restructuring of the McCain campaign and a complete change in campaign strategy. He let go almost all of his staff and decided to concentrate on winning the New Hampshire primary, hoping a win there would catapult him back into the race. With McCain seemingly out of the race in the summer of 2007, his fundraising continued to be tepid for the rest of 2007, trailing not only Romney and Giuliani but also Fred Thompson and Ron Paul in the third quarter and Paul, Romney, and Mike Huckabee in the fourth quarter.[24]

Obama and Clinton finished 2007 with roughly equal resources. However, their fundraising strategies were quite different and had serious implications for the 2008 nomination process. Clinton, as the presumptive front-runner for the nomination, concentrated on raising as much money as possible in as large amounts as possible—essentially trying to get as many donors as possible to give the maximum amount allowed under federal election law ($2,300 in 2008). In each of the four quarters of 2007, between two-thirds and three-fourths of Clinton's contributors gave the legal maximum to her campaign.[25] Obama, on the other hand, focused at least part of his fundraising strategy on raising contributions in smaller donations, and online. In part this strategy was predicated on the fact that Obama didn't have the donor base that Clinton had, so he couldn't assume that donors would give the maximum to his campaign. In 2007 only in the second quarter did more than half of Obama's contributions come from such donors. In the other three quarters of 2007, less than half of Obama's contributions came from these donors.

Had Clinton wrapped up the nomination on February 5, as many observers assumed she would, her fundraising strategy would have been successful. However, when she didn't wrap up the nomination, she found herself without a ready base of donors to go back to for what would be an arduous nomination fight. After the New Hampshire primary, both Clinton and her husband were told by Harold Ickes, a senior campaign adviser, that "the cupboard is empty."[26] Clinton lent her campaign $5 million following the New Hampshire primary, and twice more she lent money to her campaign during the nomination fight. Her strategy of maxing out her donors meant that, when she needed more money in the spring of 2008, she needed to find new donors. The Obama campaign, on the other hand, was able to go back to its contributors time and again, because they had not maxed out. What was also notable about the Obama campaign was the amount of money it raised through donations under $200. Over half (53 percent) of these donations during the primary were in amounts of $200 or less, compared to just a third of donations to the McCain and Clinton campaigns.[27]

By the end of August 2008 the Obama campaign had set a new fundraising record, raising $453.9 million.[28] The campaign raised twice as much money as the Clinton campaign ($220 million). The McCain campaign, raising $210 million, outraised all other Republican campaigns and twice what Mitt Romney raised ($105 million). In total, the 2008 presidential nomination process was the most expensive in U.S. history; Democratic and Republican Party candidates, combined, raised $1.2 billion and spent $1.1 billion.

Apart from the sheer amount of money raised during the 2008 nomination period, the other noteworthy fact is the discrepancy between the amounts raised by Democrats and Republicans. Democratic candidates, beginning in the first quarter of 2007 and continuing through 2008, outraised Republican candidates. There was simply more enthusiasm in 2008 for Democratic candidates than for Republican candidates, and that played out in terms of fundraising, as well as electoral turnout.

The 2008 general election was the first election since enactment of the Federal Campaign Act of 1971 in which a major party candidate did not accept public funding in the general election. Obama's fund-raising success in 2007 continued into 2008. He raised $55 million in February, $40 million in March, $31 million in April, and $21.9 million in May.[29] While the McCain campaign's 2008 fundraising total considerably exceeded that of 2007, particularly once McCain became the presumptive Republican nominee in March, it still did not reach that of the Obama campaign. The McCain campaign came close to parity with the Obama campaign in May, raising $21.8 million, and increased its fundraising over the amounts raised in March ($15.4 million) and April ($18.5 million). Yet despite increased fundraising success in the spring of 2008, the McCain campaign was in no position to turn down public funding in the general election.

The Obama campaign's fundraising completely dominated the McCain campaign during the general election. By the time of the Democratic Convention in late August, Obama had raised $77 million for the general election.[30] The campaign raised $150 million in September, and another $115 million between October 1 and Election Day. In the end, the Obama campaign raised $750 million during the primary and general elections, far surpassing the fundraising success of both of his competitors in 2008 and any previous presidential candidate.

The 527 organizations that played a role in the 2004 elections were not players in any significant way in the 2008 presidential election, for several reasons. First, the Obama campaign discouraged the formation of 527 organizations on behalf of its campaign. The Obama campaign wanted to control its campaign message, and because 527 organizations cannot coordinate with campaigns, the Obama campaign did not want any outside group acting in ways that might not fit with the strategies of the campaign. Also, because of the campaign's fundraising successes, it was able to run its own voter contact and get-out-the-vote operations and did not need to rely on outside groups, as Kerry had in 2004.[31] On the Republican side, John McCain had long been an opponent of 527 organizations, so it was hard for his supporters to get much traction in raising money for such organizations. However, as a result of a U.S. Supreme Court decision in early 2010, it is likely that 527 organizations will again play a role in the 2012 election.

CONCLUSION

Between 1968 and 2008 the campaign finance system in presidential elections almost went full circle. In 1968 and 1972 there were virtually no limits on what candidates could raise and spend. Following the Federal Election Campaign Act of 1971 and the amendments to the act in 1974, the costs of presidential campaigns were constrained and were increased only marginally between 1976 and 1996. Beginning in 2000, when George W. Bush decided not to accept partial public funding during the nomination period, and continuing in 2004, when neither major party nominee accepted partial public funding, the costs of seeking the nomination skyrocketed. Finally, in 2008 the costs of both primary and general elections reached historic amounts.

The difference between 1968 and 2008, however, was the way money was raised. In 1968 and 1972, large corporate and individual contributions were the norm. Corporate money was not a part of the campaign finance picture in 2008, and the most money an individual could contribute was $2,300 in the primary and $2,300 in the general. Moreover, with the advent of Internet fundraising in 2000, small individual contributions played an increasingly important role in presidential campaign funding. The financing of presidential elections had become much more democratic in the forty years between 1968 and 2008: campaign donations were smaller and were fully disclosed, and mechanisms were in place to allow donors to give in ways more accessible to them and to the campaigns.

CHAPTER TWO

THE NOMINATION PROCESS

THE FORTY YEARS BETWEEN 1968 and 2008 saw a profound change in the way the Democratic and Republican Parties nominate their candidates for president. For much of the nation's history the nomination process was controlled by political parties. Delegates to the national nominating conventions were chosen by state conventions controlled by party and elected officials—usually mayors, governors, and senators.[1] In 1968, as opposition to the Vietnam War raged in the United States, the makeup of the delegates to the Democratic convention began to show signs of the changes to come. Theodore White describes the delegates to the 1968 Democratic Convention:

> By and large, the majority of the delegates were the kind of men and women who had always come to American conventions—middle-aged, established in their parties, their unions, in civic responsibility, in high office. . . . But among them was an entirely new leaven, the delegates of the new mood of 1968, for whom the convention was not only business, but crusade. . . . The insurgents had come to Chicago to bring an end to old politics.[2]

In an effort to appease the antiwar protesters at the Democratic Convention, those angry that Hubert Humphrey was nominated without entering a single primary or caucus, the Democratic Party established a commission to examine its nomination process.[3] The Commission on Party Structure and Delegate Selection, informally known as the McGovern-Fraser Commission (after its cochairs, Senator George McGovern and Minneapolis mayor Donald Fraser), recommended a series of reforms to the nomination process to ensure that the nomination process was more inclusive and diverse. As a result of the rules changes first implemented during the 1972 nomination process and continued in subsequent years, the nomination process changed from one dominated by backroom politics to one much more open and transparent.

DEMOCRATIC PARTY REFORMS

The Democratic Party established a series of reform commissions between 1968 and 2008—the McGovern-Fraser Commission following the 1968 elections, the Mikulski Commission following the 1972 elections, the Winograd Commission following the 1976 elections, the Hunt Commission following the 1980 elections, and the Commission on Presidential Nomination Timing and Scheduling following the 2004 elections. The commissions addressed four major issues: how to increase and ensure diversity among the delegates, the commitment of delegates to candidates at the convention, the role of elected officials and party figures, and the timing of the nomination process.

Affirmative Action

The first of these issues, increasing diversity among convention delegates, was the main focus of the first reform commission, the McGovern-Fraser Commission. The main contribution of this commission to reforming the nomination process was opening up the nomination process to demographic groups largely excluded from the process throughout most of the history of the United States. The commission mandated that state party organizations ensure that the proportion of young people, women, and African Americans in each state's delegation to the convention were representative of the state's general population—in essence, requiring quotas for women, African Americans, and young people in each state's delegation.[4]

The reforms recommended by the McGovern-Fraser Commission were instituted by the Democratic Party at its 1972 nominating convention. The 1972 convention was the most open and most diverse convention in the party's history. Forty percent of the delegates were women (compared to 13 percent at the 1968 convention), 15 percent were African American (compared to 5 percent in 1968), and 23 percent were between the ages of eighteen and twenty-nine (compared to just 3 percent in 1968). Jeane

Kirkpatrick, in her study of delegates to the 1972 Democratic Convention, notes that while the McGovern-Fraser Commission "increased the numbers of women, blacks and youth in the national convention and open[ed] the party to new faces and ideas . . . it also produced a convention whose majority did not reflect and was not responsive to the values, views and policy preferences of most Democrats or most voters."[5]

As a result of the outcome of the 1972 presidential election, in which the party's nominee, George McGovern, received only seventeen Electoral College votes, the Democratic Party established another reform commission, the Mikulski Commission, named after its chair, Senator Barbara Mikulski, to consider additional reforms to the nomination process. The Mikulski Commission eliminated the use of quotas in the delegate selection of women, young people, and African Africans but still retained a commitment to affirmative action in the selection of minority and women delegates to the convention.

Following the 1976 election the Democratic Party once again addressed the issue of affirmative action in state delegations to the national convention. The Winograd Commission, chaired by Morley Winograd, chair of the Michigan Democratic Party, required that affirmative action programs for state delegations include "specific goals and timetables" for representation at the convention of minorities, which were defined as women, African Americans, Hispanics, and Native Americans.[6] While the Winograd Commission did not require the delegates to be equally divided between men and women, the Democratic National Committee did institute such a requirement for the 1980 convention.

The Hunt Commission, established after the 1980 convention, continued to address the issue of affirmative action. This commission recommended the continuation of the affirmative action criteria established by the Winograd Commission but also continued the mandate that the DNC had established for the 1980 convention that state delegations to the Democratic National Convention have equal numbers of women and men.[7] The Hunt Commission's recommendations largely settled the democratization of the delegates to the Democratic Convention begun with the McGovern-Fraser Commission and amended by the Mikulski and Winograd Commissions. From 1984 on, state delegations to the Democratic National Committee were required to have equal representation of men and women and to aspire to affirmative action for minorities.

The 2008 delegates to the Democratic National Convention kept to this requirement of gender parity and ethnic and racial diversity. Almost one quarter of the delegates were African American, and 11 percent were Latino.[8]

Delegate Candidate Preferences

The McGovern-Fraser Commission also addressed the relationship between convention delegates and the candidates. The commission recommended that delegates state their candidate preference or their uncommitted status.[9] The commission also discontinued the unit rule, which allowed a majority of a state's delegation to cast all of the delegation's votes for one candidate.

The Mikulski Commission established the "candidate right of approval rule," which gave presidential candidates the right to approve of all delegates committed to them.[10] The Winograd Commission strengthened the requirements for delegates' candidate preferences, requiring that delegates elected to support a specific candidate vote for that candidate on the first ballot at the convention (the "bound delegate rule"). The Hunt Commission subsequently removed the bound delegate rule but retained the provision established by the Mikulski Commission that candidates could approve individual delegates. The assumption was that candidates would only approve delegates who would vote for them on the first ballot. For conventions in which the party's nominee was known well ahead of time, this provision meant little, but for those conventions in which the outcome was less certain, the voting intention of convention delegates was much more important.

Role of Elected and Party Officials

The third issue the Democratic nomination process reforms addressed was the role of elected and party officials in the official nomination process. Through the 1968 nomination elected officials and party officials essentially determined the party's nominee. Elaine Kamarck describes this process:

> Every four years, local party officials, precinct leaders, ward leaders, county chairmen, and others would participate in a series of meetings throughout their state that usually culminated in a state

convention. At that point the assembled party leaders would choose a group of (mostly) men to attend the national nominating convention. If the state party happened to be controlled by a particularly powerful party "boss," often a big-city mayor, a governor, or a senator, he would have sole discretion in the selection of delegates. If there was no dominant party leader, the selection of delegates would be privately negotiated by party officials and elected leaders.[11]

This is exactly the process that was in place at the 1968 Democratic Convention, despite the presence at the convention of delegates who had been elected in support of Eugene McCarthy, Robert Kennedy, and George McGovern. Hubert Humphrey and Chicago mayor Richard Daley controlled the convention and thus the nomination. As Theodore White describes it, "The Humphrey delegates were the old structured vote. Humphrey had entered no primaries . . . but the AFL-CIO structures had delivered to him almost all of Pennsylvania, Maryland, Michigan and Ohio; Democratic governors and mayors . . . could deliver hundreds more delegates from New Jersey to Washington. . . . All in all, the mechanics of the Humphrey delegate control had been well and competently handled."[12]

The McGovern-Fraser Commission began to address the control of the nomination process by party bosses by, first, requiring that only 10 percent of a state's delegates to the convention could be selected by the state party, and second, requiring that those delegates be elected within the calendar year of the convention.[13] (Some of Humphrey's delegates to the 1968 convention were originally Lyndon Johnson delegates, chosen in 1967 before Johnson dropped out of the presidential race.)[14] The commission also prohibited ex officio delegates, that is, those individuals not elected as convention delegates but attending the convention in their official capacity as an elected official or party leader.[15] The Mikulski Commission began the slow expansion of the role of party and elected officials, though they never again achieved the power they had in the past. The Mikulski Commission expanded the percentage of delegates who could be selected by the state party committee from the 10 percent established by the McGovern-Fraser Commission to 25 percent; it also granted convention privileges to Democratic governors, representatives, senators, and Democratic National Committee members, with the understanding that this group of delegates could not vote at the convention.[16]

The Winograd Commission allowed each state at-large delegates equal to 10 percent of the state's delegation.[17] Some party officials thought that, while the McGovern-Fraser reforms had opened up the nomination process, the reforms had also created a system that allowed the nomination of candidates who could not win in the general election (George McGovern in 1972) or were largely unknown to party officials (Jimmy Carter in 1976).

After Jimmy Carter's unsuccessful reelection campaign in 1980, the Hunt Commission further expanded the role of elected and party officials in the nomination process. The commission required that 14.4 percent of the total number of delegates be reserved for elected and party officials and further required that these delegates be technically uncommitted to any one candidate. These uncommitted party and elected officials quickly became known as superdelegates. The role of superdelegates would be to "enhance and encourage the review of prospective presidential candidates by their party peers during the nomination period" and to "provide a built-in voice for those who presumably knew the candidates best and would have to work with the nominee should he be elected to the presidency."[18] In other words, they would ensure that candidates like Jimmy Carter were not nominated in the future.[19] Between 1984 and 2004 the superdelegates in fact played little if any role in the selection of the party's nominee. In 2008 their potential for influencing the outcome of the nomination became much more important.

Timing of the Nomination Process

The Winograd Commission was the first reform commission to address the timing of the nomination process. One consequence of the requirements of the McGovern-Fraser reforms was that more and more states moved from caucuses and conventions to primaries as a way to elect convention delegates. Not only did the McGovern-Fraser reforms require more diversity in state delegations, but the reforms also had provisions for more transparency in the way delegates were selected.[20] In 1972, the first year of the reforms, twenty-one states held primaries; four years later, in 1976, the number of states holding primaries instead of caucuses and conventions had increased to thirty.[21]

The Winograd Commission established a nomination process that started on the second Tuesday in March and ended on the second Tuesday in June, with exceptions for states where state law requires primaries or caucuses to be held outside the March-June window. In practice that meant that Iowa retained its position as the first caucus state and that New Hampshire remained the first primary state. The Commission on Presidential Nomination Timing and Scheduling, established after the 2004 election, returned to the issue of the timing of the nomination; its recommendations are discussed later in this chapter.

REPUBLICAN PARTY REFORMS

The reforms of the Democratic Party nomination process were driven by the perceived exclusiveness of the process both before and including the 1968 elections. Because the Republican Party was more homogeneous, there was not the drive for reform within the party. Nevertheless, there were two Republican Party reform commissions, one before the 1972 convention and one subsequent to the convention. The Delegates and Organization (DO) Committee, formed in 1969, came up with general recommendations that proposed more transparency in the delegation selection process and an effort by the state parties to seek equity in the numbers of men and women in state delegations to the convention.[22] However, unlike the Democratic Party reforms, there was no requirement that the state parties adopt the recommendations and no sanctions for noncompliance. Following the 1972 convention the Rule 29 Committee was created to address the question of minority representation in state delegations to the convention. However, because at the time the policies of the Republican Party were not particularly attractive to minorities, there was no simple way to develop an affirmative action program. In the end, the Republican National Committee encouraged state delegations to take "positive action" to include minorities, but as with the DO Committee, there were no sanctions for noncompliance.

While the Republican reform committees had little effect on the composition of the delegates to the nominating conventions, the reforms of the nomination process instigated by the Democratic Party nevertheless spilled over into the Republican Party. As more and more states abandoned caucuses for primaries, the Republican nomination process, like the Democratic process, became more primary driven. States simply did not want the extra time and expense of different nomination processes for Republican and Democratic candidates.

PROPORTIONAL REPRESENTATION VERSUS WINNER TAKE ALL

While the evolution from a primarily convention and caucus nomination process to a primary system affected both the Democratic and Republican Parties relatively equally, the way delegates are assigned as the result of primaries and caucuses differs between the two parties, and the different rules can dramatically affect the nomination process and its outcome. The Democratic Party uses a proportional representation system to assign delegates to candidates, meaning a candidate who receives 15 percent or more of the votes in the primary or caucus receives a number of that state's delegates proportional to his or her vote in the state. The Republican Party uses a variety of methods to assign delegates to candidates, including a winner-take-all system, which means that the candidate who receives a plurality of the state's vote receives all of the state's delegates.

The Democratic Party eliminated winner-take-all systems at the state level beginning in 1976. While some states used methods to select delegates other than proportional representation between 1976 and 1988, by 1992 all delegates to the Democratic National Convention were elected by proportional representation.[23]

In contrast, the Republican Party uses a variety of methods to elect delegates to the national convention, including proportional representation, winner-take-all by state, winner-take-all by congressional district, direct election of delegates (meaning votes are cast for the delegates themselves, not the candidate to whom they are committed, though that candidate's name usually appears on the ballot as well), and, in some states, a combination of proportional representation and winner take all.[24] This disparity in the way delegates are allocated can lead to significant differences in the way the nomination process unfolds in each party, as is shown later in this chapter.

THE POSTREFORM NOMINATION PROCESS

While the post 1968 reforms had little effect on the Republican nomination in 1972, they had a major effect on the Democratic nomination process. The number of primaries increased from seventeen in 1968 to twenty-one in 1972, and the share of delegates elected in primaries increased from 42 percent in 1968 to 63 percent in 1972.[25] At the start of the nomination process in 1972 Senator Edmund Muskie, the vice presidential nominee in 1968, was seen as the front-runner. However, Senator George McGovern, the cochair of the McGovern-Fraser Commission that wrote the new delegate selection rules, understood the implications of the increased number of primaries and the requirements for more diversified delegations. By the time of the last primary in New York in June, McGovern had effectively locked up the Democratic nomination, even though Muskie was the favorite of the Democratic establishment, as evidenced by the number of endorsements he received from party leaders. McGovern went on to lose every state but Massachusetts and the District of Columbia to President Richard Nixon in the general election and, as we saw above, sent the Democratic Party back to the drawing board to tweak their nomination process.

In 1976, 1980, and 1984 candidates seeking the nomination were able to use the nomination window, in combination with partial public funding of the nomination process, to contest the nomination from the Iowa caucuses and New Hampshire primary through the nomination contests held between March and June. Georgia governor Jimmy Carter finished second to "undecided" in the Iowa caucuses, despite heavy campaigning in the state, yet did at least 10 percent better than any other Democratic candidate.[26] Following the Iowa caucuses Carter methodically worked his way toward the nomination. He gained momentum in New Hampshire, and it was obvious that Carter was a serious contender when he finished virtually tied in the Oklahoma primary with Senator Fred Harris, an Oklahoma native. Although he had a disappointing showing in important states such as Massachusetts, Carter finally locked up the nomination in June. In 1984 Colorado senator Gary Hart was able to use the nomination process and campaign finance rules to contest the nomination with the front-runner, Vice President Walter Mondale. Early in his candidacy Hart ranked fifth of six candidates in terms of fundraising. Hart's surprising second-place finish to Mondale in the Iowa caucuses provided momentum going into the New Hampshire primary, which he comfortably won. His fundraising eventually improved, with the help of matching funds, and he out-campaigned all other contenders. He narrowly defeated Mondale in California but lost to him in New Jersey, and between the last primaries in June and the start of the Democratic convention Mondale claimed enough delegates to get the nomination.

Carter and Hart are just two examples of lesser known candidates using the combination of reformed campaign finance and nomination rules to contest the nomination throughout the nomination period. Former California governor Ronald Reagan challenged President Gerald Ford for the nomination throughout the nomination period in 1976, Massachusetts senator Ted Kennedy fought Carter for the nomination throughout the nomination period in 1980, and in 1988, though Massachusetts governor Michael Dukakis essentially wrapped up the nomination in March, the Reverend Jesse Jackson still contested the nomination into the summer months. One consequence of the 1970s reforms was the enhanced importance of the Iowa caucuses and the New Hampshire primary to the outcome of the nomination process. While Iowa and New Hampshire had long been the first nomination contests, their importance was muted when the nominations were decided by party officials, out of the public eye. However, as primaries became more the norm, the nomination process became more public. Beginning with Carter's success in the Iowa caucuses in 1976, more and more attention was paid to these early contests, particularly by the media.

As Iowa and New Hampshire gained prominence in the nomination process, more states sought to emulate states with early nomination contests. While the window created by the Winograd Commission prohibited states from moving their primaries and caucuses earlier than the first Tuesday in March, beginning in 1980, a number of states began to move their election contests into March. In 1980, 35 percent of the delegates to the Democratic National Convention were chosen in March, compared to just 17 percent four years earlier. The biggest increase in delegates chosen in March occurred between 1984 and 1988. The primaries and caucuses on March 8, 1988, were referred to as Super Tuesday, when twenty-two states held their primaries and caucuses.[27]

The 1988 nomination was also notable because it was the first attempt to establish a regional primary. In 1985 a group of southern political leaders proposed a regional southern primary, to try to give the South more influence in the selection of the party nominee.[28] Their efforts came to fruition in 1988; on March 8, 67 percent of the delegates to be elected were from southern states.[29] While the southern strategy didn't lead to the nomination of a southerner in 1988—two liberal candidates, Massachusetts governor Michael Dukakis and the Reverend Jesse Jackson were the most successful Democratic candidates on March 8, and Dukakis went on to win his party's nomination—the southern regional primary in 1988 set the stage for Arkansas governor Bill Clinton's successful nomination fight in 1992.

Super Tuesday in 1988 set the stage for the front-loading of the nomination process. States saw the influence they could have on the nomination process by moving their primaries and caucuses to the front of the nomination process. For the 2000 nomination process the Republican Party moved up the window for the selection of delegates from the first Tuesday in March to the first Monday in February, and the Democratic Party had no choice but to go along, though the earlier window didn't have much effect on the Democratic nomination process until 2004. By 2008 almost half the states held primaries or caucuses on Super Tuesday, February 5; there were twenty-two Democratic primaries and caucuses and twenty-one Republican primaries and caucuses that day. Combined with the primaries and caucuses that were held in January, 60 percent of the delegates to the Democratic Convention and 55 percent of the delegates to the Republican Convention were chosen by the first Tuesday in February, a far cry from the three-month delegate selection process put in place by the reform process forty years earlier.

The Democratic National Committee tried to address the problem of front-loading in 2004. The DNC appointed the Commission on Presidential Nomination Timing and Scheduling to look at the timing of the nomination contests. The impetus for forming the commission came from Michigan Senator Carl Levin, who argued that the prominence of Iowa and New Hampshire in the nomination process hindered the influence of manufacturing states such as Michigan. While Iowa and New Hampshire had long held influence as the first two nomination contests, Iowa and New Hampshire were not seen as representative of most of the United States. Both states are small and have overwhelmingly white populations. Senator Levin argued that a state such as Michigan had much more diversity in terms of both its demographic makeup and its economic issues.

The commission recommended that the window for the nomination process in 2008 begin on February 5 and end on June 10. The commission exempted Iowa and New Hampshire from the window and recommended that no nomination contests occur before January 14 and that the DNC Rules and Bylaws Committee add one or two primaries and caucuses to the prewindow period occupied by Iowa and New Hampshire.[30] To specifically address the front-loading issue, the commission recommended no more than five contests a week, with an incentive for states that held their nomination contests later in the nomination period. The commission also recommended dividing the nomination process into four stages (March 4 to March 17, March 18 to April 7, April 8 to April 28, and April 29 to June 10) and adding additional delegates to states within each stage, ranging from 15 percent more delegates to states in the first stage to 40 percent more delegates to states in the fourth stage. Republicans attempted a similar process in 2000, awarding states a certain percentage of additional delegates (5 percent, 7.5 percent, and 10 percent) if they held their contests after March 15, April 15, and May 15, respectively.

In practice, the Democratic Commission's attempt to reduce front-loading in the 2008 nomination process had no effect. States were much more interested in the attention drawn to them by an early contest than additional delegates awarded if they held their contests later in the primary season. However, the commission's recommendations that additional states be added to the Iowa and New Hampshire prewindow did have important implications for the 2008 nomination calendar. To address the lack of demographic diversity in Iowa and New Hampshire, the DNC's Rules and By-Laws Committee recommended that South Carolina, a southern state with a large African American population, and Nevada, a western state with a large Latino population as well as a large union presence in the casinos in Las Vegas, be added to the pre-February 5 window. The Rules and By-Laws Committee set the following dates for the 2008 primaries and caucuses: Iowa caucus, January 14; Nevada caucus, January 19; New Hampshire primary, January 22; and South Carolina primary, January 29; all other primaries and caucuses were to be held within the nomination window beginning on February 5.

By spring of 2007 it became clear that the initial primary and caucus schedule was going to be difficult for the political parties to follow. In May the Florida Republican Party decided to move its primary from March 11 to January 29, and the Democratic Party, because of a local initiative on the ballot, decided to move its primary as well. In August 2007 the South Carolina Republican Party announced that it would move its primary from January 29 to January 19 in order to maintain its status as the first southern primary. The DNC Rules and By-Laws Committee met in August and voted to strip Florida of its delegates to the Democratic National Convention the following summer, arguing that by scheduling the Florida primary outside the permissible window, the Florida Democratic Party violated the party's nomination rules.

As mentioned above, the impetus for the DNC's Commission on Presidential Timing came from Michigan senator Carl Levin, in an effort to give Michigan more of a role in the early nomination process. When that didn't happen, and Nevada and South Carolina were moved into the prewindow instead of Michigan, Senator Levin worked with the Michigan Democratic Party to move the Michigan primary to January 15.[31] In December the DNC's Rules and By-Laws Committee took the same action it had against the Florida Democratic Party, stripping Michigan of its delegates to the Democratic Convention in 2008.

With the Michigan primary on January 15, just one day after the original date for the New Hampshire primary, the question became what would happen to the New Hampshire and Iowa nomination contests. At one point there was speculation that one or both contests would be held in December 2007. In the end, Iowa moved its primary to January 8, and Iowa moved its caucus to January 3. Instead of four nomination contests in January (Iowa, Nevada, New Hampshire, and South Carolina), there were six Democratic contests (Iowa on January 3, New Hampshire on January 8, Michigan on January 15, Nevada on January 19, South Carolina on January 26, and Florida on January 29), and seven Republican contests (Iowa, New Hampshire, Michigan, Nevada, and Florida on the same dates as the Democratic contests, plus Wyoming on January 5 and South Carolina on January 19).

THE 2008 NOMINATIONS

The nomination process in 2008 bore little resemblance to the nomination process forty years earlier. The majority of delegates were chosen in the first month of the nomination process, and that first month was no longer March, or even February, but January, that is, January 3 to February 5. Yet even though the majority of delegates were chosen in the first two months, the quest for the nomination, at least for Democrats, once again extended into June, allowing a less well known candidate, Barack

Obama, to challenge the front-runner, Hillary Clinton, and to eventually win the nomination.

The Republicans

While John McCain was seen as the presumptive front-runner entering the prenomination process in 2007, his abysmal fund-raising in the first and second quarters of 2007 left him with a skeletal staff and, many thought, little chance of winning the nomination. McCain decided to forgo the Iowa caucuses and concentrate his efforts in New Hampshire, a primary McCain had won in 2000. In New Hampshire, independents (technically called *undeclared voters*) can vote in either the Democratic or the Republican primary, and in 2000 they voted overwhelmingly for McCain.[32] McCain hoped that independents would come forward for him again in 2008.

Rudy Giuliani decided to begin his nomination quest in Florida, forgoing not only Iowa and New Hampshire but also Wyoming, Nevada, and South Carolina. Giuliani hoped that the nomination field would be sufficiently splintered that there would be no clear front-runner going into the Florida primary on January 29 and that a win in Florida would give him momentum going into Super Tuesday on February 5. That left Mitt Romney, Mike Huckabee, and Fred Thompson to contest the Iowa caucuses.

Romney had easily won the Republican Iowa straw poll in August of 2007 and was the perceived front-runner going into the January caucuses.[33] However, Huckabee, who had finished a surprising second in the Iowa straw poll the previous summer, convincingly defeated Romney in the caucus, winning 35 percent of the vote, compared to Romney's 25 percent, with Fred Thompson finishing third, with 13 percent of the vote.[34] Romney hoped his proximity to New Hampshire, as the former governor of Massachusetts, would give him an advantage in the New Hampshire primary, but McCain's willingness to bet on New Hampshire coming through for him once again paid off, and McCain won the New Hampshire primary with 37 percent of the vote, compared to 32 percent for Romney and just 11 percent for Mike Huckabee.[35]

While McCain and Romney split the Republican vote, independents once again supported McCain, just as they had in 2000.[36] Romney finally got his first primary win in the Michigan primary but lost to McCain in both South Carolina and Florida. Going into Super Tuesday on February

5, McCain led the delegate count with 93 delegates, compared to Romney's 59 delegates.[37] However, because of the winner-take-all rules in a number of Super Tuesday states, including Arizona, California, and Missouri, McCain emerged from Super Tuesday with 704 delegates, over half of the 1,191 delegates needed for the nomination, while Romney had only 247 delegates. Though it would be another month before McCain officially became the presumptive nominee of the Republican Party, locking up the nomination on March 4, the Republican nomination process was essentially over on February 5, just thirty-two days after it began. Romney dropped out of the race and endorsed McCain on February 7. Giuliani didn't even make it to Super Tuesday; he ended his candidacy and endorsed McCain following the Florida primary.[38] (Huckabee stubbornly continued his candidacy through the March 4 primaries.)

The Democrats

When the contest for the 2008 Democratic nomination began in earnest in early 2007, the assumption was that Senator Hillary Clinton would be the Democratic nominee. She had easily won reelection to her Senate seat in 2006, had access to a large fundraising network, and had wide name recognition and a tested campaign organization. As far back as 2006 *Weekly Standard* editor and *New York Times* columnist Bill Kristol predicted that "if [Hillary Rodham Clinton] gets a race against John Edwards and Barack Obama, she's going to be the nominee."[39] The first meeting of the fledgling Obama campaign focused on Clinton's inevitability. David Plouffe, the Obama campaign's manager, describes that discussion:

> Barack did ask questions about the politics, and to a person we said that Hillary Clinton was an enormously strong front-runner. In fact, at this point, it was hard to see how she could lose. . . . She was the eight-hundred-pound gorilla, with organizations in every state, 100 percent name recognition, and a fund-raising machine ready to be switched on at a moment's notice. We had none of this. Nothing, nada, zilch. Any political conversation about the 2008 primaries started and ended with Hillary Clinton.[40]

Senator McCain also assumed Hillary Clinton would be the Democratic nominee. On one of his early forays into New Hampshire in the spring of 2006, McCain reflected on a Clinton candidacy: "She's smart. She's tough. She's disciplined. . . . I could probably imagine a couple of remote scenarios where she doesn't get the nomination, but in most scenarios, she's got the nomination."[41] Even the Clinton campaign was confident she would be the Democratic nominee. When asked at a post-election conference in 2008 about the Clinton campaign's thinking going into 2007, Howard Wolfson, the campaign's communications director, said that "we had a fair amount of confidence that she would be the nominee."[42] Wolfson went on to say that the goal of the Clinton campaign in the prenomination period was "to project inevitability."

While the nomination was still seen as Clinton's to lose as the caucuses and primaries began, two factors suggested that her nomination might not be inevitable. One was Obama's fundraising success in 2007. The second was Obama's clear position against the war in Iraq, a position he had staked out as early as 2002.[43]

By the spring of 2007 support for the war in Iraq among Americans had declined precipitously, and Obama was the candidate who most clearly articulated opposition to the war.[44] In a speech at an antiwar rally in Chicago in October of 2002, Obama came out clearly against the Iraq War.[45] A *Washington Post* poll in late November 2007 foreshadowed what was to happen in Iowa a little more than a month later. The poll suggested that "the factors that have made Clinton the clear national front-runner . . . do not seem to be translating on the ground in Iowa."[46] That poll showed that among likely caucusgoers, 30 percent would support Obama, 26 percent would support Clinton, and 22 percent would support John Edwards, the third top-tier candidate as the formal nomination process began.

The Iowa caucuses provided the first chink in Clinton's inevitability. Obama won 38 percent of the delegates, Edwards finished second with 30 percent of the delegates, and Clinton finished third with 29 percent of the delegates. With his win in Iowa, Obama proved that an African American candidate could win support in a state with an overwhelmingly white population. With the Iowa caucuses began the long, drawn-out battle for the Democratic nomination. Senator Clinton bounced back to win the New Hampshire primary just five days after losing the Iowa caucuses and won the Nevada caucuses on January 19. However, Obama won the South Carolina primary on January 29, just a week before the February 5 Super Tuesday contests.

Going into the February 5 primaries and caucuses Obama had 63 delegates, Clinton had 48, and Edwards had 26, closer than the McCain, Romney, Huckabee race on the Republican side but, as with the Republicans, making for a competitive race for the nomination. However, because of the proportional representation rules of the Democratic Party, no clear front-runner emerged after February 5. Clinton was ahead in delegates but by less than 100 delegates (Clinton had 814 delegates through February 5, and Obama had 766). Had the states that were winner take all for Republicans also been winner take all for Democrats, Clinton would have had almost twice the number of delegates (1,026) as Obama (554), and most likely the Democratic nomination, like the Republican nomination, would have been effectively decided after Super Tuesday.

The strategic assumptions of the Clinton and Obama campaigns influenced how the nomination process played out and, ultimately, the nomination itself. The Obama campaign knew it had to win Iowa to have any chance at winning the nomination. In his book, *The Audacity to Win,* David Plouffe said, "It started and ended with Iowa. If we did not win there, our chances were probably zero."[47] However, the campaign thought that if it was successful in Iowa the nomination rules, particularly proportional representation, and the nomination calendar, particularly the addition of a South Carolina primary before Super Tuesday, could be used to boost Obama's chances of winning the nomination. Because about half of the primary electorate in South Carolina was African American, the Obama campaign thought it had a chance to win the South Carolina primary and give the campaign valuable momentum going into Super Tuesday.

Plouffe also committed about $5 million in resources for the Super Tuesday states, so that if Obama won in Iowa there would be organizational resources in place to allow Obama to compete on Super Tuesday.[48] When Obama came out of Super Tuesday still in the race, the Obama campaign saw the fight for the nomination as a battle for delegates. To that end, the campaign focused on caucus states like Idaho, which—while they would be carried by a Republican in the general election—still would send delegates to the Democratic Convention. The Clinton campaign, in contrast, saw the nomination as a battle for states, not delegates, and put its resources into winning large states and states that would likely be battleground states in the general election, such as Ohio and Pennsylvania.

One example illustrates the success of the Obama strategy and the problems with the Clinton strategy. New Jersey, a Democratic state in the general election, held its primary on February 5, and Idaho, a Republican state in the general election, also held its caucus that same day. There were 107 delegates at stake in New Jersey and just 18 in Idaho. Clinton convincingly carried New Jersey, winning 54 percent of the vote, but because of proportional representation received 59 delegates; Obama received 48. Obama won the Idaho caucus with 79 percent of the vote and picked up 15 of the 18 delegates. Between the two states Clinton picked up 62 delegates; Obama picked up 63.[49]

Because of this nomination strategy of the Obama campaign and the proportional representation rules of the Democratic Party, the presumptive nominee of the Democratic Party was not decided until the Montana and South Dakota primaries on June 3, when Barack Obama picked up 76 delegates, to give him 2,152 delegates, 34 delegates more than the 2,118 needed to secure the nomination.

Superdelegates had not played a role in the nomination process until 2008. Because of Obama's successes in the primaries and caucuses following Super Tuesday (he won eleven straight contests following Super Tuesday; Clinton did not have another win after Super Tuesday until March 4), he developed a lead in pledged delegates. While the battle between Clinton and Obama for pledged delegates continued through the primaries and caucuses from March to June, there was also a battle for the approximately 800 superdelegates who would attend the convention.

Before the Iowa caucus Clinton surpassed Obama in superdelegates by over a hundred, but following Super Tuesday she surpassed him by less than a hundred.[50] As discussed above, the Clinton campaign's strategy was to win in large states that would be battleground states in the general election. That became Clinton's argument to superdelegates: she would be the stronger candidate against McCain in the general election. The Obama campaign, in turn, argued to superdelegates that they should support Obama because "they should not override the popular will of Democratic voters."[51] In the end, Obama prevailed. By May the Obama campaign "was locking down superdelegates at a ratio of 5 or 6 to 1."[52] On June 3, the last day of the primaries, the Obama campaign calculated that it needed only a few more superdelegates to clinch the nomination, and during that day more and more undeclared superdelegates announced their support for Obama. Obama ended up with about two-thirds of the superdelegates.[53] The role of superdelegates at future Democratic Party Conventions would become a point of discussion as the Democratic Party considered reforms to the nomination process before the 2012 election.

PRENOMINATION PROCESS

The front-loading of the nomination process and the declining reliance on partial public funding for the nomination meant that the prenomination process became increasingly important. Nowhere was this more important than in campaign finance. As discussed in chapter 1, George W. Bush learned from the experiences of Robert Dole in 1996 and decided that, for his presidential bid in 2000, he would eschew partial public funding. His fundraising success in the second quarter of 1999 ($35 million) reduced the Republican nomination field before a single primary or caucus vote was cast. Four years later, Howard Dean's fundraising successes in 2003 led him to turn down partial public funding during the nomination process, and John Kerry felt that to be competitive, he too needed to fund his nomination bid with private contributions. During the prenomination period for the 2008 election the expectation was that a candidate, to be competitive in the nomination fight, would need to raise $100 million in 2007; both Barack Obama and Hillary Clinton did just that. While the Republican candidates were not as successful, both Mitt Romney and Rudy Giuliani raised more than the 2008 primary spending limit in 2007.

The need to raise funds meant that candidates had to begin their presidential campaigns earlier and earlier. Both the 2000 and 2004 elections were well under way a year before any primary votes were cast. The 2008 election began before the 2006 congressional elections ended. The first straw poll for the Republican presidential candidates was held in March 2006 in Memphis, Tennessee. A month later John McCain attended a fundraiser for state legislators in Concord, New Hampshire, Hillary Clinton's advisers started putting together a strategy for a presidential campaign in the summer of 2006, and Barack Obama first met with his advisers to discuss a presidential run the day after the 2006 congressional elections.[54]

The 2012 presidential elections got an even earlier start than the 2008 elections. In June 2009 Minnesota governor Tim Pawlenty announced he would not seek reelection in 2010 and in September formed a political action committee; both moves were widely seen as the beginnings of a 2012 presidential run.[55] Pawlenty's hiring of several former advisers to John McCain's presidential campaign and his creation of an Internet team in October of 2009, combined with trips to Iowa in November and New Hampshire in December, further fueled anticipation of Pawlenty's run for the presidential nomination.[56]

Pawlenty was not the only potential Republican presidential candidate whose actions in 2009 drew attention from the press and political operatives. Former Massachusetts governor and 2008 Republican presidential candidate Mitt Romney's fundraising on behalf of Republican candidates in 2009 furthered speculation that he would again be a candidate in 2012.[57] Mississippi governor Haley Barbour's trips to Iowa and New Hampshire in the summer of 2009 led to speculation that he too was considering a 2012 presidential race.[58] By the end of 2009 Pawlenty, Romney, and Barbour, plus 2008 Republican vice presidential nominee Sarah Palin, former Arkansas governor and 2008 presidential candidate Mike Huckabee, former House Speaker Newt Gingrich, and former Pennsylvania senator Rick Santorum were all considered potential 2012 Republican presidential candidates.[59] Eighteen months later, Barbour and Huckabee had decided not to run, and Palin was still considering whether or not to enter the race. Pawlenty, Romney, Gingrich, and Santorum, though, were all declared candidates.

CONCLUSION

Between 1968 and 2008 the nomination process evolved from one dominated by party activists and largely held behind closed doors to one in which nominees are chosen largely in public primary elections. The Democratic Party process, once spread out over four months and narrowing later to front-loading in February and March, expanded to six months. Following the 2008 nomination process both the Democratic and Republican Parties formed commissions to examine the nomination process and address some of the issues caused by front-loading. The recommendations of those commissions and the nomination rules for 2012 are discussed in chapter 8.

CHAPTER THREE

THE NOMINATING CONVENTIONS

THE TUMULTUOUS 1968 DEMOCRATIC Convention and the lack of transparency in the nomination of Hubert Humphrey led to the reforms of the nomination process. And it was not just the nomination process that changed; the nominating conventions themselves also changed, evolving from being the culmination of the nomination process to becoming the kickoff of the general election. As the nomination process changed and the presumptive presidential candidates for each party became known well before the nominating conventions, the historical role of the conventions—deliberation among the delegates to select the party's presidential candidate—changed. However, the conventions still play an important role in the presidential election process, as this chapter describes.

The most important role of the nominating conventions has been to select the party's presidential and vice presidential candidates. Between 1832, when the first nominating convention was held by the Democratic Party, and 1952, convention delegates, chosen by state and local party leaders, met to choose the party's presidential nominee. Stephen Wayne describes how these conventions worked: "Prior to 1956, conventions were decision-making bodies. Majorities were constructed within them to nominate presidential candidates. Party leaders, who exercised considerable control over the selection of their state delegation, debated among themselves. Once they agreed on the candidate, they cast the votes of their delegates in favor of their particular choice."[1]

While conventions still convene to formally choose each party's nominee, the conventions of the 1970s and 1980s were far different from those in the nineteenth century and earlier in the twentieth century. At those earlier conventions multiple ballots were often necessary before the nomination was secured. For example, at the Democratic Convention in 1924, 103 ballots were cast before the nominee was decided.[2] Multiple ballots last occurred at the Republican Convention in 1948, when it took three ballots for Thomas Dewey to capture the nomination, and at the Democratic Convention four years later, in 1952, when it also took three ballots for the nominee, Adlai Stevenson, to be chosen.[3] By the latter part of the twentieth century the party's nominees were largely known before the start of the conventions. While no major party candidate failed to get his party's nomination on the first ballot between 1968 and 2008, candidates continued to face challenges to their nominations through 1988.

Three party committees, the Rules, Credentials, and Platform Committees, also play important roles at the conventions. In attempts to change the outcome of the nomination process in the years following the 1968 conventions, it was often through these committees that candidates who had been unsuccessful in the primary process attempted to capture their party's nomination. The vice presidential selection process also changed in the four decades between 1968 and 2008. As the nomination of the presidential candidates, the roles of the Rules, Credentials, and Platform Committees, and the vice presidential selection process changed between 1968 and 2008, the conventions themselves moved from being tumultuous gatherings like the Democratic Convention of 1968 to being carefully scripted like the conventions of 2008.

NOMINATION CHALLENGES

The first serious nomination contest following the first reforms to the nomination process occurred at the 1976 Republican Convention, when the former California governor Ronald Reagan tried to take the nomination away from President Gerald Ford. In his efforts to gain the nomination, Reagan took the unprecedented step of announcing his vice presidential selection, Pennsylvania senator Richard Schweiker, before the start of the convention. Reagan hoped that the addition of the more liberal Schweiker to the ticket would provide a broader base of support for his candidacy. Reagan tried to change convention rules to force Ford to also announce his vice presidential selection before his name was formally placed in nomination.

The Democratic Party saw a challenge to its sitting president at the 1980 convention, when Senator Ted Kennedy challenged the nomination of President Jimmy Carter. Anticipating Kennedy's challenge, Carter's supporters implemented a change to the convention rules, requiring delegates to vote for the candidate they had supported during the primaries. Kennedy tried to get the rule overturned, to create an "open convention" and give him an opportunity for the nomination. In the end Kennedy's challenge was unsuccessful, but the dissent within the Democratic Party was clear coming out of the convention.[4]

In 1988 Jesse Jackson finished second to Michael Dukakis in the delegate count before the convention began. While Jackson publicly congratulated Dukakis on his victory following the final primary contests in June, privately he and his aides were plotting a way to keep Jackson's agenda front and center at the Democratic Convention, including "asserting influence on the party platform and rules reform, as well as the candidate's chances to be on the ticket."[5] Dukakis never seriously considered Jackson as his vice presidential nominee, even though Jackson continued to press Dukakis right up to the convention.

Challenges to party nominees occurred several times between 1976 and 1988, but by 1992 candidates came out of the nomination process sure that they would not face challenges at the conventions. Bill Clinton was not challenged at the Democratic Convention in 1992 and 1996, nor were Al Gore in 2000, John Kerry in 2004, and Barack Obama in 2008. George H. W. Bush faced no challenges in 1988 nor did his son, George W. Bush, in 2000 and 2004. John McCain had no opposition in 2008. As the inevitable nominees became clear before the conventions, convention challenges ceased.

CREDENTIALS CHALLENGES

The Credentials Committee is responsible for deciding if the state delegations to the parties' conventions are selected following the delegate selection rules established by the parties. At the 1968 Democratic Convention there were credentials challenges to fifteen state delegations, many of them based on the racial composition of the delegations.[6] At the 1964 convention the party had prohibited racial discrimination in the selection of state delegations, yet several of the southern delegations to the

1968 convention faced credentials challenges along racial lines. As the Democratic Party worked to implement the diversity requirements of the McGovern-Fraser Commission, it was the Credentials Committee that had to decide if the state delegations met the diversity requirements specified in the reforms.

At the 1972 Democratic Convention, the party grappled with not only continued racial challenges to some delegations but also the implementation of the delegate apportionment requirements of the McGovern-Fraser Commission. There were eighty-two credentials challenges at the 1972 convention, representing more than 40 percent of total delegates.[7] Perhaps the most controversial challenge was that to the California delegation. California in 1972 had a winner-take-all primary, and George McGovern had won the primary. The question arose over whether the banning of the unit rule at the 1968 convention prohibited winner-take-all primaries. The Credentials Committee ruled that it did, but this ruling was later overturned by a vote of the entire convention.[8]

Credentials challenges abated at the 1976 and 1980 Democratic Conventions. At the 1984 Democratic Convention Senator Gary Hart considered challenging some of the Mondale delegates but decided before the convention actually started not to pursue the challenges.[9] From 1988 forward, as the nomination process became more open and delegates more diverse, credentials challenges all but disappeared at the Democratic Conventions. For Republicans, credentials challenges at the conventions were never really an issue, due to the more homogeneous characteristics of the delegates.

CONVENTION DELEGATES

Between 1968 and 2008 delegates to the conventions became more diverse, most noticeably in the Democratic Party, although there were also changes in the delegates to the Republican Conventions. As table 3-1 shows, the biggest change in both parties was an increase in female delegates. In 1968 over 80 percent of the delegates to both conventions were men; by 2008 women had reached parity with men at the Democratic Convention and were a third of the delegates to the Republican Convention.

The percentage of African Americans and Latinos at the Democratic Conventions also increased markedly between 1968 and 2008. African

TABLE 3-1. Convention Delegates, 1968–2008
Percent

	1968	1972	1976	1980	1984	1988	1992	1996	2000	2004	2008
Democrats[a]											
Male	87	60	67	51	51	52	52	50	52	50	51
Female	13	40	33	49	49	48	48	50	48	50	49
African American	5	15	11	15	18	23	16	19	19	18	23
Latino	*	*	*	5	6	6	7	9	12	12	11
Asian	*	*	*	1	2	2	*	3	3	3	3
Ages 18–29	3	23	15	11	8	4	4	6	4	7	7
Republicans[b]											
Male	84	71	69	71	56	67	57	64	61	56	68
Female	16	29	31	29	44	33	43	36	35	43	32
African American	2	4	3	3	4	4	5	3	4	6	2
Latino	*	*	*	1	4	3	4	3	6	7	5
Asian	*	*	*	*	*	*	2	1	2	2	2
Ages 18–29	4	6	7	5	4	3	*	2	3	4	3

a. CBS/*New York Times* Delegate Poll, August 24, 2008.
b. CBS/*New York Times* Delegate Poll, August 31, 2008.
*Not asked in this year's survey.

Americans made up just 5 percent of the delegates to the 1968 Democratic Convention, a share that rose to almost 25 percent by the 2008 convention. The percentage of Latinos at the conventions more than doubled between 1980 and 2008, increasing from 5 percent in 1980 to 12 percent in 2000 and 2004 and 11 percent in 2008. Minority representation at the Republican Conventions did not change much during the time period, reflecting the identification of minorities with the Democratic Party.

Table 3-1 also shows the increase in young people attending the Democratic Conventions following the McGovern-Fraser Commission recommendations. Almost one-quarter of the delegates to the 1972 convention were between the ages of eighteen and twenty-nine. However, young people represented only 15 percent of the delegates to the 1976 convention and barely 11 percent of the delegates to the 1980 convention. At the more recent conventions their numbers hovered between 4 and 7 percent.

At the Republican Conventions young people, like minorities, were less represented than at the Democratic Conventions.

RULES CHALLENGES

The democratization of the nomination process came about not only because of changes in the composition of state delegations to the conventions but also because of changes to party rules. The first major rule change of the modern era occurred at the 1968 Democratic Convention, when the unit rule was abolished. The unit rule required all members of a state's delegation to support the candidate of the majority of the delegates. Because the delegates to the conventions were largely selected by party leaders, the unit rule meant, in practice, that party bosses could control the votes of their states' delegates.[10]

As seen from the discussion above, what the abolishment of the unit rule for voting at the convention meant for the selection of delegates was a major topic for the Rules Committee at the 1972 Democratic Convention. The McGovern-Fraser Commission required that state delegations be reflective of state populations, particularly with respect to gender, race, and age. However, it was up to the Rules Committee at the 1972 Democratic Convention to figure out exactly how to create rules to implement the commission's requirements. As mentioned, the convention faced a record number of credentials challenges, as the Credentials Committee tried to figure out if state delegations were selected in accordance with the guidelines of the McGovern-Fraser Commission.

The main conflict centered on the issue of winner take all versus proportional representation in the selection of delegates. Because the McGovern-Fraser Commission report had not used the term *proportional representation* but instead used the term *fair reflection,* it was not clear that banning the unit rule at the convention also meant banning winner-take-all primaries.[11] After much discussion, the Rules Committee at the 1972 Democratic Convention voted that proportional representation would be the norm for the selection of delegates to future Democratic Conventions.[12] However, it took a series of reform commissions and debates within Rules Committees at the Democratic Conventions between 1976 and 1988 for proportional representation to finally, at the 1992 convention, become the only method for selecting delegates.

While the Republican Conventions in 1968 and 1972 had no serious rules challenges, a major rules fight erupted at the 1976 Republican Convention. As noted earlier, Ronald Reagan was seeking to wrest the nomination away from President Gerald Ford, and he thought one way to do so would be to require Ford to name his vice presidential choice before his formal nomination. Reagan thus proposed a change in the rules to require a presidential nominee to name his vice presidential nominee before his name is placed in nomination. The proposed change in the rules was defeated, but just barely.[13]

A rules challenge was also used at the 1980 Democratic Convention to try to change the outcome of the primaries. Massachusetts senator Edward Kennedy had unsuccessfully challenged President Jimmy Carter for the nomination. Earlier in 1980 President Carter and his supporters had gotten the Democratic National Committee to enact a rule (Rule F3(c)) requiring that delegates be bound to vote for the candidate they supported during the nomination process.[14] At the convention Senator Kennedy and his supporters tried to overturn Rule F3(c) to create an "open convention" and, hopefully, to nominate Kennedy. Kennedy's effort, like Reagan's four years before, was unsuccessful; Carter prevailed by over 500 votes and became the formal nominee of the Democratic Party. There were no significant rules challenges at the Democratic or Republican Conventions after 1980, as both parties became more comfortable with the nomination process put in place by the various reform commissions of the 1970s and 1980s.

Platform Challenges

As delegates to the conventions became more diverse, so did their views on the party platform. Formally, the party platform represents the views of the party on policy issues. It is the responsibility of the Platform Committee to draft the platform, and the committee tries to do so out of the spotlight of the full convention. However, between 1968 and 1996 both the Democratic and Republican Conventions saw disagreements about the platform spill onto the convention floor.

Not surprisingly, given the acrimony at the 1968 Democratic Convention, a major platform fight ensued over a minority report involving the war in Vietnam. The report included a call for the "cessation of bombing of North Vietnam" and "a negotiated withdrawal of American troops."[15] Also, not surprisingly, given Hubert Humphrey's control of the convention, the report was defeated, giving more fodder to the antiwar forces protesting Humphrey's nomination.

At the 1972 Democratic Convention Alabama governor George Wallace offered challenges to the party platform. Wallace wanted planks in the platform to outlaw busing to integrate schools, to support tax reform, to reintroduce the death penalty, to require school prayer, to support the right to own guns, and to cut back federal aid to states. He also wanted the party to support the election of federal judges as well as require the reconfirmation of Supreme Court justices.[16] All of his challenges were defeated with simple voice votes. Other minority reports showed the new, more diverse interests of the convention delegates that year. One report proposed a government guaranteed annual income for a family of four (27 percent of the delegates to the convention had incomes under $10,000, compared to just 13 percent of the delegates to the 1968 convention); another supported abortion rights. Both were defeated, though the abortion rights plank was defeated by less than 500 votes.[17]

The Republican Convention in 1972 and both parties' conventions in 1976 had no major platform fights, but platform fights threatened to disrupt the 1980 Democratic Convention. The diversity mandated by the McGovern-Fraser Commission was in full force by the 1980 convention. Representation of African Americans, Latinos, Native Americans, Asian Americans, and gays was substantially higher than it had been at the convention just four years earlier.[18] In Platform Committee meetings before the start of the convention there were at least thirty-six minority reports. To ward off lengthy debates and roll call votes on each of the minority reports, Carter and Kennedy negotiated a confidential agreement to allow just five reports to be brought before the full convention. Despite the Carter-Kennedy agreement, female delegates, now half of the delegates to the convention, still forced votes on two minority reports particularly important to them—Medicaid funding for abortions and withholding of financial support and campaign assistance by the party for candidates who didn't support the Equal Rights Amendment. With support from teachers and African Americans, both reports were accepted by voice vote.

The 1980 Republican Convention also faced the possibility of a contentious platform fight. While the Democratic Party was being pushed by the left wing of the party, the Republican Party was being pushed by its conservative wing on the issue of abortion. A platform subcommittee had drafted language prohibiting the appointment of Supreme Court justices who did not publicly state their opposition to abortion, opposing federal funding of abortions for poorer women, and opposing the Equal Rights Amendment. To avoid a fight over these issues on the floor of the convention, a compromise was reached that stated that the Republican Party supported a constitutional amendment "to restore protection of the right to life for unborn children," supported "congressional efforts to restrict the use of taxpayers' dollars for abortion," and would "work for the appointment at all levels of the judiciary of judges who respect traditional family values and the sanctity of innocent human life."[19]

Platform challenges occurred at both conventions again in 1984. Both Gary Hart and Jesse Jackson offered minority reports to the Democratic Party's platform. While the Mondale forces on the Platform Committee were able to defeat most of these challenges, they did accept a Hart-sponsored report on the use of unilateral military involvement in the Persian Gulf and a Jackson-sponsored plank on affirmative action.[20] At the Republican Convention, conservative elements were successful in getting language into the platform that prohibited abortion, denied homosexuals rights, supported school vouchers and voluntary school prayer, and supported stricter antipornography laws.

The 1988 and 1992 conventions were without major platform challenges in either party. In 1996, however, the Republican Convention had a contentious battle over the party's stance on abortion. Bob Dole, the party's presumptive nominee, held a relatively moderate position on abortion and wanted to include "tolerance language" in the platform that "described abortion as a manner of personal conscience and recognized the deeply held and sometimes differing views on the issue."[21] Antiabortion delegates on the Platform Committee, however, repeatedly defeated attempts to moderate the party's position on abortion, and the 1996 Republican platform once again called for a constitutional amendment to ban abortions.[22] Between 2000 and 2008 no significant platform challenges occurred in either party.

For Democrats the conflicts were between the moderate and liberal wings of the party on issues such as abortion, women's rights, and affirmative action. For Republicans the split was between the moderate and conservative wings of the party largely over social issues such as abortion and school prayer. However, as the party conventions became even more scripted in 2000, 2004, and 2008, these platform challenges, if they existed at all, were resolved within the Platform Committees and beyond the scrutiny of the full conventions.

VICE PRESIDENTIAL NOMINATIONS

For much of the country's history, vice presidential candidates were chosen at the nominating conventions, following the nomination of the party's presidential candidate. Ronald Reagan broke that precedent at the 1976 Republican Convention when he announced, before the convention, that were he to be the party's nominee he would choose Pennsylvania senator Richard Schweiker as his vice presidential running mate.

With the exception of 1976, the Republican Party continued the practice of selecting the vice presidential candidate at the convention until 1996, when the presumptive Republican nominee, former senator Robert Dole, named former New York congressman and secretary of Housing and Urban Development Jack Kemp as his running mate the day before the start of the convention. Democrats moved away from selecting the vice presidential nominee at the convention in 1984, when Walter Mondale announced, days before the start of the convention, that he had selected New York representative Geraldine Ferraro. Since 1996 both parties' presumptive presidential nominees have announced their vice presidential selections before the start of the convention. In most cases the nominee was announced within a week of the convention, though in 2004 John Kerry announced his selection of John Edwards almost three weeks before the convention.[23]

The nomination is often timed to create positive media attention for the announcement and, by inference, for the ticket. For example, in 2008 Barack Obama announced that he would send a text message to his supporters telling them of his vice presidential selection. Word of the selection leaked but only hours before the text message was sent. In 2008 John McCain, hoping to take some of the momentum away from Barack

Obama's acceptance speech at the Democratic Convention, announced his selection of Sarah Palin the day after Obama's speech. In fact, word of Palin's selection leaked to the media early Friday morning, taking away almost all media discussion of Obama's speech the night before.

Traditionally, the vice presidential candidate is selected to balance the presidential ticket in terms of demographics, regional base, or political experience. Ronald Reagan, George H. W. Bush, Michael Dukakis, George W. Bush, and Barack Obama all chose vice presidential candidates for their political experience. In 1980 former California governor Ronald Reagan chose George H. W. Bush as his vice presidential nominee. Bush had been the chairman of the Republican National Committee, chief of the U.S. Liaison Office in the People's Republic of China, and director of Central Intelligence, so his national and international experience complemented Reagan's experience at the state level. In 1988 Massachusetts governor Michael Dukakis chose Texas senator Lloyd Bentsen to balance the ticket in terms of experience. He felt that, as a governor, he wanted someone on the ticket "with credentials as a Washington insider and on foreign policy issues."[24] In 2000 Texas governor George W. Bush also turned to someone with Washington experience, choosing Dick Cheney as his vice presidential nominee. Cheney had served as secretary of Defense in President George H. W. Bush's administration, had been a member of the House of Representatives for ten years, and had served as chief of staff to President Gerald Ford. In 2008 Barack Obama, who was in his first term in the U.S. Senate when he received his party's presidential nomination, chose Senator Joe Biden, a thirty-five-year veteran of the Senate, as his vice presidential running mate. As the chair of the Senate Foreign Relations Committee, Biden brought balance to the ticket in terms of foreign policy experience, which Obama, as a first-term senator, lacked.

Ticket balancing in terms of candidate demographics is common, though not in terms of gender. In 1984 Democratic presidential candidate Walter Mondale took the unprecedented step of trying to achieve gender balance on the ticket by choosing Representative Geraldine Ferraro to be his vice presidential nominee. Ferraro was the first woman nominated by a major party to be vice president. A more common demographic in play is age. In 1988 sixty-four-year-old George H. W. Bush chose forty-one-year-old Dan Quayle as his vice presidential nominee. Twenty years later, John McCain, then seventy-two years old, chose forty-four-year-old Sarah Palin as his running mate.

The Dukakis-Bentsen team of 1988 is one example of an attempt at regional balance, as is the 1960 candidacy of Senator John Kennedy of Massachusetts and Senator Lyndon Johnson of Texas.

In 1992 Democratic nominee Bill Clinton broke from the tradition of ticket balancing when he chose Senator Al Gore as his running mate. Clinton and Gore were approximately the same age, and both were from the South (Clinton from Arkansas and Gore from Tennessee). By choosing Gore, Clinton was trying to send a message that the Clinton-Gore ticket was young and dynamic, in contrast to the older President Bush, running for election after serving as vice president under President Reagan, the oldest president in U.S. history.

CHANGES IN MEDIA COVERAGE

While television coverage of national party conventions first began in 1948, it was in 1952 that television coverage became widespread.[25] That year the three networks televised roughly 60 hours of coverage of each party's convention, and American households watched an estimated ten to thirteen hours of each convention. Estimates are that somewhere between a third and a half of the country watched the conventions. In 1968 television coverage of the Democratic Convention was interspersed with coverage of the confrontations between protestors and police in Grant Park. The coverage hurt the positive image of the party and its nominee that parties try to portray at conventions. As early as 1960 the networks had begun to work with the Democratic and Republican Parties to shape the convention to the needs of television. The unfavorable coverage of the Democratic Convention in 1968 heightened the desire for the parties to stage conventions to show the party and its nominee in a favorable light.

In 1968 the gavel-to-gavel coverage of conventions that had begun in 1952 began to change. ABC covered only one-quarter of what it had televised in 1964, and by 1980 both NBC and CBS had also ceased covering the entire convention.[26] By 1984 coverage of the conventions by all three networks was just a sliver of what it had been in the 1950s and 1960s.[27]

As the purpose of the conventions moved from actually deciding the nominee to introducing the nominee to the general electorate, the parties tried to script conventions to present the party and its nominee in a favorable light. Zachary Karabell describes how this worked at the Republican Convention in 1972:

> The Republicans micromanaged every detail of their convention, with the aim of presenting a predetermined image of the party and its candidate Richard Nixon. Each night was scripted by party officials and copies of the scripts were provided to the networks, complete with minute-by-minute details of music, applause and the movements of the speakers. Also included was a candidate film, during which the hall lights were dimmed . . . with the lights dimmed and no other activity, the parties effectively forced the networks to air them in full.[28]

The Democrats were not as successful in scripting their 1972 convention; George McGovern, the party's nominee, gave his acceptance speech at three in the morning in Miami.

Scripted conventions didn't always play to a party's advantage. At the Republican Convention in 1992 the party's conservative leanings were fully displayed. While the convention may have solidified the party's base, it probably hurt the image of the party with the general electorate. In subsequent years the Republican Party tried to script its convention to show the inclusiveness of the party.

As the conventions became more scripted, they also became less newsworthy, so the networks, while understanding they still had to provide some coverage, continued to cut back on it. In 1996 Ted Koppel, then anchor of ABC's *Nightline* program, took his camera crew and left the Republican convention, saying that it "wasn't worth it."[29] There were more newsworthy stories for *Nightline* to cover.

The rise of cable television meant that, even if the three networks reduced their coverage of conventions to only an hour of prime time, there were still outlets for viewers who wanted to see more of the conventions. However, cable coverage of conventions is much different from the traditional coverage provided by the networks. Cable coverage tends to be dominated by commentators discussing the proceedings, or even discussing topics only tangentially related to what is actually happening at the convention, rather than showing the proceedings themselves. A study comparing network and cable coverage of the Democratic and Republican Conventions in 2004 finds that less than 7 percent of cable news coverage focused on what was happening at the convention podiums, compared to 80 percent of network coverage.[30] Moreover, cable coverage of the podium was often taped sound bites, while the network coverage was more likely to be live.

CONCLUSION

The historic role of the party nominating convention—to deliberate and to select the party's presidential nominee—had ceased by 1968. Instead, party nominees were determined in the primaries and caucuses that preceded the conventions. However, party conventions continued to play an important role in working out party differences about delegates to the conventions and party platform issues. Between 1968 and 2008 delegates to the conventions became more demographically diverse and, as a result, so did the issues discussed at the conventions. The conventions became not the end of the nomination process but the beginning of the general election and a vehicle for the general electorate to view each party's nominee.

The decline in network coverage also sharpened what the parties presented to viewers and what viewers watched. Record numbers of viewers tuned in to watch the acceptance speeches of the Democratic and Republican candidates in 2008: 38.4 million people watched Obama's acceptance speech, more than the number that watched the opening ceremonies at the Olympics, the Academy Awards ceremony, or the final episode of *American Idol* that year.[31] A week later, 38.9 million watched McCain accept his party's nomination.[32] The Democratic and Republican Conventions in 2008 were the most watched nominating conventions in history.[33]

CHAPTER FOUR

THE GENERAL ELECTION

THREE EVENTS CHARACTERIZE THE evolution of presidential general elections between 1968 and 2008. The first is the winnowing of states that candidates campaign in. Between 1968 and 2008 the number of contested states declined, until only a dozen or so states see fervent campaign activities; the majority of states are considered noncompetitive for one party or the other. The second is the return of presidential debates. After the 1960 Kennedy-Nixon debates candidates eschewed debates for several election cycles. The debates returned in 1976 and by 1988, with the creation of the Commission on Presidential Debates, became an established part of the general election. The third event is the 2000 election, only the fourth election in the history of the United States in which the winner of the popular vote did not win the Electoral College vote. The protracted legal fight to determine the winner of that election involved the court system in a way that had never happened before. The fight ended only with a decision by the U.S. Supreme Court.

BATTLEGROUND STATES

National party conventions now mark the beginning of the general election campaign, considered to be the time period between Labor Day and Election Day (the first Tuesday after the first Monday in November). In 1960 presidential candidate Richard Nixon famously boasted at the Republican National Convention that he would campaign in all fifty states in the general election; John F. Kennedy had visited all fifty states during the spring of 1960.[1] But the period between 1968 and 2008 saw a narrowing of states in which candidates actually campaign.

What makes the presidential general election in the United States unique from any other U.S. election is the Electoral College. The president is not elected by a national popular vote but by a majority of Electoral College votes. Each state is assigned Electoral College votes equal to the number of senators and representatives from each state; the smallest states have 3 Electoral College votes (1 for each of the two senators and 1 for the at-large member of the House of Representatives), while the most populous state, California, has 55 Electoral College votes. The passage of the Twenty-Third Amendment in 1961 gave the District of Columbia 3 Electoral College votes. The fifty states plus the District of Columbia combined have 538 Electoral College votes. To be elected president, a candidate needs a majority of these votes, or 270.

A candidate who wins a plurality of the popular votes in each state receives all of the state's Electoral College votes, with two exceptions— Maine and Nebraska. In those two states the candidate who wins the plurality of the state's popular vote receives two Electoral College votes; the other votes are assigned to candidates based on the popular vote in each congressional district. In 2008 in Nebraska John McCain won 57 percent of the statewide vote, as well as the popular vote in the First and Third Districts, but Barack Obama carried the Second District, and thus Nebraska's Electoral College vote was split, with four votes for McCain and one for Obama.[2]

With 270 Electoral College votes needed for the nomination, candidates, as early as 1968, began to evaluate how to put together states to achieve that Electoral College majority. Richard Nixon realized in his 1968 presidential campaign that campaigning in all fifty states, as he had promised to do in 1960, was not the optimal strategy. His 1968 Electoral College strategy was not about inclusion, as it had been in 1960, but about selecting so-called battleground states that the campaign would focus on. Theodore White described Nixon's strategy in 1968 as follows:

In 1968, the strategy began by elimination. "We couldn't lose Arizona," said Peter Flanigan. . . . Similarly with the farm states and certain Rocky Mountain states—they were solid for Nixon, no point in wasting battle effort there. On the other end of the spectrum were states like Massachusetts—it was impossible, Nixon's private polls said, for him to carry Massachusetts. . . . There remained then, a number of major states and several border states where the race would be won or lost.[3]

The 1968 election introduced the notion of battleground states. While such states would change over the ensuing forty years, the idea that candidates would campaign in only certain states to get them to 270 Electoral College votes would become a staple of presidential campaign strategy. In 1968 Richard Nixon, learning from his mistakes in 1960, concentrated on states with large electoral votes—New York, Pennsylvania, New Jersey, Ohio, Michigan, Texas, Illinois, Wisconsin, Missouri, and California—which together came close to the 270 votes needed to win the election. However, the 1968 election was complicated by the presence of a third-party candidate, former Alabama governor George Wallace, who was popular in the South. Because Nixon couldn't be assured he would win all ten targeted large states, he had a contingent strategy that focused on states that were unlikely to vote for Hubert Humphrey but might support Wallace. These states—Florida, North Carolina, Virginia, Tennessee, and South Carolina—became the true battleground states in the 1968 election, the states that would determine the outcome of the election.[4] In the end, Nixon won six of the targeted big states and all five of the targeted southern states.[5]

The strategy of targeting specific states to reach 270 Electoral College votes became the norm for campaigns following the 1968 election. Going into the 1980 general election President Jimmy Carter's pollster, Pat Cadell, identified the key battleground states for Carter as Ohio, Pennsylvania, Illinois, Texas, Michigan, New Jersey, Wisconsin, California, New York, Florida, and Missouri. Richard Wirthlin, Ronald Reagan's pollster, identified the battleground states for the Reagan campaign as California, Illinois, Texas, Ohio, Pennsylvania, New York, and Michigan.[6]

The deliberative process to win the Electoral College vote is well illustrated by the Republican Party's presidential strategy in the 1988 election. The party's electoral strategy began in 1987, before the party's nominee was known.[7] In 1987 Frank Fahrenkopf, then chair of the Republican National Committee, met at first every two weeks, and then once a week, with a top campaign official for each candidate thinking about seeking the Republican nomination. The group decided to focus on twenty-five states with a total of 362 electoral votes; the other twenty-five states would be ignored—no time, money, or other resources would be spent in those states.

The assumption was made that, in the twenty-five states that would be the focus of the campaign, the Republican candidate would get 40 percent of the vote and the Democratic candidate would get 40 percent. This assumption came from the fact that, even in a party's worst presidential years, each party's candidate had come close to 40 percent of the vote. In 1964 Republican presidential nominee Barry Goldwater received only fifty-two Electoral College votes, but 38.5 percent of the popular vote. In 1972 Democratic presidential nominee George McGovern received just seventeen Electoral College votes, but 37.5 percent of the popular vote, and in 1984 Walter Mondale carried just his home state of Minnesota and the District of Columbia, with a total of thirteen Electoral College votes, yet he got 40.6 percent of the popular vote.

The Republican National Committee and the presidential campaigns decided to direct their resources to gaining 20 percent of the vote in the twenty-five targeted states; they needed 11 percent of the 20 percent to win those states' Electoral College votes (the 40 percent assumed base vote plus 11 percent equaled 51 percent). The RNC surveyed residents in those targeted states and asked if they considered themselves liberal or conservative on three issues: foreign policy, defense, and the domestic economy. The survey found that 5 percent of the respondents were self-identified conservatives and 2 percent were self-identified liberals. Combining the survey results with the assumed 40 percent base vote gave the Republicans a new base vote of 45 percent (40 percent assumed plus 5 percent of self-identified conservatives) and the Democrats a new base vote of 42 percent (40 percent assumed plus 2 percent of self-identified liberals). With a 45 percent base vote, the Republican candidate needed just 6 percent of the vote in the targeted states to win the Electoral College.

While the early battleground states included the most populous states—California, New York, and Texas—between 1980 and 2000 states became more and more categorized by their vote history, and these large states became part of one party or the other's base states. In 1988 California and Texas were still considered battleground states by both the Dukakis and Bush campaigns. While the Bush campaign rated New

York as a leaning-Democratic state, the Dukakis campaign still considered New York a battleground state.[8] However, just four years later, both California and New York were considered base Democratic states, and Texas had moved into the lean-Republican column.

In 1992 the Democratic presidential nominee, Bill Clinton, divided the Electoral College map into four categories: top end, play hard, big challenge, and watch only. There were thirteen top-end states, plus the District of Columbia, for a total of 182 Electoral College votes. These were states that the Clinton campaign thought they could win fairly easily; they included California, New York, and Illinois. There were eighteen play-hard states, with a total of 194 Electoral College votes; these were the states where the campaign thought the election would be decided and, together with the top-end states, equaled 376 Electoral College votes. There were ten big-challenge states—states the campaign didn't think were winnable for Clinton—with 63 Electoral College votes; these states included Indiana, Virginia, and Utah. The final category, the watch-only states, had 99 Electoral College votes and included—interestingly, given what happened in the 2000 election—Florida. In the end, Clinton carried all the top-end states and all but one of the play-hard states (he lost North Carolina, another state that would come into play in a later presidential election). He won one big-challenge state, Nevada, again a precursor of a future election, and ended up with 370 Electoral College votes.

With the most populous states, and those with the most Electoral College votes, falling into the base states for each party, campaigns began to craft electoral strategies to get them to 270 Electoral College votes with a combination of large and small states. Daron Shaw, a strategist for the Bush campaign in 2000, describes the approach Karl Rove, Matthew Dowd, and others in the Bush inner circle took to their electoral college strategy in 2000 as "dichotomous. . . . States were either in play or not. States that Gore had carried would get minimal resources, while states that had gone Democratic in 1996 but were designated battlegrounds for 2000 would get significant attention."[9] Battleground states were prioritized according to six criteria: "past statewide voting history, contemporaneous polling numbers, organizational development and endorsements, other hot races in the state or solid top-of-the-ticket candidates, favorable issue environments in the states, and native son effects." While there was an initial list of twenty-nine battleground states, in practice the campaign narrowed the list of true battleground states to fifteen: Arkansas, Florida, Iowa, Maine, Michigan, Minnesota, Missouri, New Hampshire, New Mexico, Oregon, Pennsylvania, Tennessee, Washington, West Virginia, and Wisconsin. Estimates are that the Gore campaign targeted thirteen states as true battleground states, the same states that the Bush campaign targeted, except for Minnesota and West Virginia.

In targeting its states for the 2004 election the Bush campaign focused on the weakest performing Bush and Gore states in 2000. There were six of each; the states Bush carried in 2000 that were targeted in 2004 were Florida, New Hampshire, Missouri, Ohio, Nevada, and West Virginia. States that went Democratic in 2000 that Bush targeted in 2004 were New Mexico, Wisconsin, Iowa, Oregon, Minnesota, and Maine. In addition, because of their past voting history, Pennsylvania, Michigan, and Wisconsin were added to the targeted list. That made a total of fifteen states, the same number as 2000, and thirteen of the fifteen states were the same states targeted in 2000. Arkansas and Tennessee were dropped from the list of targeted states, and Ohio and Nevada were added.[10] As the election drew closer, Missouri, Maine, and Washington were moved from the list of targeted states and reclassified as lean Bush (Missouri) and lean Kerry (Maine and Washington). Estimates are that the Kerry campaign had seven key targeted states: Florida, Iowa, New Hampshire, New Mexico, Ohio, Pennsylvania, and Wisconsin.

Of the twenty-five states targeted by the Republican Party in the 1988 election, there were less than a dozen in which the 2004 election was focused. In both 2000 and 2004 the election came down to one state—Florida in 2000 and Ohio in 2004. In 2008 the Obama campaign sought to expand the battleground states. They thought they had a chance to compete in states that had fallen into the Republican column in 2000 and 2004, and they also wanted to develop an electoral college strategy that gave them more than one winning strategy. David Plouffe said,

> We did not want to wake up on the morning of November 4 dependent on one state, as Kerry was on Ohio in 2004 and to a lesser extent Gore was on Florida in 2000. We wanted to have a wide set of targets so that we could lose some and still win the presidency. . . . In 2000 and 2004, our party was forced to have its fate rest on the outcome of one state. That would not happen in 2008.[11]

The Obama campaign calculated that if they carried all the states that Kerry had won in 2004, plus Iowa and New Mexico, they would be just six votes shy of victory.[12] In their effort to expand the playing field beyond traditional Democratic states, the Obama campaign included Virginia, North Carolina, Montana, Missouri, Indiana, Colorado, Nevada, and Florida in their list of targeted states. In the end, Obama carried all of the states that voted for Kerry in 2004 as well as the targeted states of Colorado, Florida, Indiana, Iowa, North Carolina, Ohio, Virginia, Nevada, and New Mexico. The only targeted states Obama lost were Montana and Missouri; the latter by only the tightest of margins, and the vote in Montana was much closer than it had been in 2004.

As battleground states became part of the presidential campaign vernacular, so did the characterization of states as blue states and red states and later, purple states. While the late host of *Meet the Press,* Tim Russert, denied credit for the characterization of states as red and blue, the first documented reference to states as red or blue was in an exchange between Russert and NBC *Today Show* host Matt Lauer days before the 2000 general election, when Russert asked the question, "So how does [Bush] get those remaining sixty-one electoral red states, if you will?"[13] While in fact in elections between 1976 and 2000 the media had used graphics that depicted Republican states as blue and Democratic states as red, the protracted outcome of the 2000 election, and the accompanying commentary, cemented Republican states as red states and Democratic states as blue states. Moreover, the terms came to refer not just to the voting patterns of the states but also to the lifestyles of those who lived in the states. These supposed distinctions were brought home by Barack Obama, in his keynote address to the Democratic National Convention in 2004, when he tried to dispel these distinctions when he said, "We coach Little League in blue states, and we have gay friends in red states. We pray to an awesome God in blue states, and we don't like federal agents sniffing around our libraries in red states." But the fact that he described the states as he did suggests how descriptive the terms had become as a shorthand for lifestyles.[14]

THE DEBATES

The Kennedy-Nixon debates in 1960 were the first presidential debates in the modern television era. While there had been presidential debates in both 1948 and 1956, the 1960 debates were the first televised general elections debates. There were four debates between Nixon and Kennedy, each carried by all three major networks at the time (NBC, ABC, and CBS) and each with a viewership of between 60 million and 66 million people.[15] The first debate was the most famous, because, for those who watched the debate on the relatively new medium of television, the contrast between the young and energetic John Kennedy and the tired and perspiring Richard Nixon was striking. Longtime CBS producer Don Hewitt, who produced the first debate, described Kennedy and Nixon as they arrived for the debate:

> [Nixon] banged his knee getting out of the car. He looked sort of green and sallow and unhappy. Then in walks this handsome Harvard kid who looks like a matinee idol. I said to them, "Do you want some makeup?" Kennedy, who didn't need any, said no. Nixon heard him say no and decided, I can't have makeup because it will look like I got made up and he didn't. He went off in another room and got made up with something called Lazy Shave, and looked like death warmed over.[16]

The influence of television is shown by the following: those who saw the debates on television thought Kennedy won, while those who heard the debates on radio thought Nixon won.

There were no presidential general election debates in 1964, 1968, or 1972. President Johnson did not want to debate Republican candidate Barry Goldwater in 1964. And probably because of his experiences in 1960, Richard Nixon had no interest in debating his opponents in 1968 and 1972. Presidential debates resumed in 1976, under the sponsorship of the League of Women Voters, which had been sponsoring debates at the local and state levels since the 1920s.[17] In 1976 both the incumbent president, Gerald Ford, and his Democratic challenger, Jimmy Carter, were eager to debate—Ford because he was behind in the polls by double digits, and Carter because he thought he was not well known to the American people.[18] There were three presidential debates and, for the first time, a debate between the two vice presidential candidates.

The presidential election in 1980 included a third-party candidate, John Anderson. While Republican candidate Ronald Reagan had no problem including Anderson in the debates, President Jimmy Carter refused to debate Anderson. As a result, there were only two presidential debates in 1980, one in September, between Reagan and Anderson, and a second debate in late October, just one week before the election, between Reagan and Carter. The Reagan-Carter debate was the most viewed debate in history, with just over 80 million viewers, a viewership that has not since come close to being replicated.[19]

In 1984 there were two presidential debates and one vice presidential debate, again sponsored by the League of Women Voters. While the League had made a valiant effort to sponsor the debates in 1976, 1980, and 1984, it became increasingly clear to many involved in the debate process that a more permanent structure, devoted entirely to the sponsorship of the debates, was desirable. Carter's refusal to debate John Anderson in 1980 meant that the debate between the two major party candidates almost didn't happen. In 1984 the League had to name 103 journalists to serve as debate panelists before the Reagan and Mondale campaigns could agree on 4 of them.[20]

After a series of studies and conferences, there developed a consensus that the two major political parties would be the most effective structures to administer the debates, because the parties would have influence over the candidates that an outside organization would not.[21] In 1987 the Commission on Presidential Debates was created, and the commission has sponsored the debates since 1988. The commission is a private, not-for-profit organization whose primary responsibility is to "sponsor and produce debates for the United States presidential and vice presidential candidates, and to undertake research and educational activities relating to the debates."[22] The first cochairs of the commission were the chairs of the Republican National Committee and the Democratic National Committee in 1988, Frank Fahrenkopf and Paul Kirk. Both continued as cochairs of the commission after leaving their party positions; Fahrenkopf continues as commission cochair today.

The creation of the commission ensured that the debates would become a permanent part of the presidential general election process and that no candidate could opt out of the debates as Johnson did in 1964 and Nixon did in 1968 and 1972. While front-runners, and more particularly incumbents, are often reluctant to debate, the existence of the commission made sure that the American public would see both major party candidates debate several times during the fall campaigns and, as it has evolved, the vice presidential candidates as well.

In 1988 the number of debates mirrored those in 1984, with two presidential debates and one vice presidential debate. In 1992 there were three presidential debates, as there had been in 1976, and one vice presidential debate. In 1992 there was once again a third-party candidate, Reform Party candidate Ross Perot, and both Perot and his running mate, James Stockdale, were included in the presidential and vice presidential debates.

In 1996 there were only two presidential debates, and the viewership of the two debates was noticeably lower than in previous years. With the exception of the debates in 1980, viewership of presidential debates since 1976 ranged between 62 million and 69 million viewers. In 1996 only 46 million people watched the first presidential debate and even fewer, 36 million, watched the second debate. Interest in the vice presidential debate was also unusually low that year, with only 26 million people tuning in to watch Al Gore and Jack Kemp debate. Viewership of the 2000 debates was also less than it had been between 1976 and 1992, though in 2000 there were once again three presidential debates.

Viewership increased somewhat in 2004 and 2008, though not to the levels of the earlier debates. However, the vice presidential debate in 2008, between Joe Biden and Sarah Palin, was the most watched of any vice presidential debate, with 69.9 million viewers, equal to the number of viewers who watched the second presidential debate in 1992.

While the debates do not often change people's minds, they are watched, as evidenced by the viewership figures above, and do give the American public an opportunity to view the candidates in a forum apart from the thirty-second ads that dominate the airwaves in battleground states and to view them at all in nonbattleground states. Between 1976 and 2008 the formats of the debates evolved, moving from a panel of journalists asking questions of the candidates to either just one journalist moderating a discussion between the candidates or a town hall meeting in which undecided voters ask questions of the candidates.

THE 2000 ELECTION

Any discussion of presidential elections over the past forty years would be incomplete without mention of the 2000 presidential election. This was only the fourth election in American history in which the winner of the national popular vote did not win the Electoral College vote and the only such election in the modern era. The final battleground state that year was Florida. As the evening wore on the networks first called Florida for Al Gore, then moved it back to the undecided column, then at 2:16 A.M., called the state for George Bush. However, as Al Gore was traveling in his motorcade to give his concession speech, Michael Whouley, head of the campaign's ground strategy, called William Daley, the campaign chairman, who was also in the motorcade, to tell him that the results were within one-half of 1 percent, which meant, under Florida law, there would be an automatic recount. Gore had already called Bush to congratulate him on his victory, so he had the awkward task of calling Bush to take back his concession. "'Circumstances have changed dramatically since I first called you,' Al Gore told George W. Bush. . . . 'The state of Florida is too close to call.' 'Are you saying what I think you're saying?' Bush asked brusquely, disbelievingly. 'Let me make sure I understand. You're calling back to retract that concession?'"[23]

It would take thirty-six days before the winner of the 2000 presidential election was decided. On Wednesday morning George Bush's lead in Florida, which had been 50,000 votes when Gore first conceded in the early morning hours, was down to 1,784 votes.[24] Al Gore had won the national popular vote by 48.69 percent (50,996,116 votes), compared to George W. Bush's 48.18 percent (50,456,169 votes), but neither candidate had 270 Electoral College votes. Florida's 25 Electoral College votes would decide the winner of the election.[25] The five-week battle to determine the outcome of the election brought public attention to antiquated voting procedures and led, in 2002, to the passage of an election reform law, the Help America Vote Act, to modernize state voter record keeping and voting machines. The election also saw unprecedented involvement of both the state and federal courts in a presidential election. The machinations also involved local and state officials, underscoring the way political affinities can affect election outcomes.

The problems at the ballot box were evident almost from the moment the polls opened on November 7, though the ramifications of those problems would not be evident until the early morning hours of the next day. Palm Beach County, a Democratic stronghold, experimented in 2000 with the so-called butterfly ballot, named because it had candidates'

names on two pages facing each other, joined by perforations in the
middle where voters could indicate their vote preferences by punching
through a paper chad. The first two candidates on the left side of the
ballot were George W. Bush, listed first, and Al Gore, listed second. On
the right side of the ballot, at the top, was Patrick Buchanan, the Reform
Party's candidate in 2000. What became clear over the course of the day
was that some people, thinking they were voting for Al Gore, the second
candidate on the left side of the ballot, actually voted for Pat Buchanan,
whose name was above Gore's, though on the right side of the ballot.[26]

There were numerous other ballot-related problems in Florida in
2000. Many of the ballots required voters to punch out a chad to cast
their votes. In some cases the chads weren't entirely punched out, leaving it unclear exactly what the voter intent was (so-called undervotes). In
other cases, voters were confused as to how to vote and ended up voting
more than once, thus disqualifying their votes (so called overvotes).[27]

The automatic recount showed Bush to have a lead of 327 votes.[28] The
Gore campaign requested a manual recount in four heavily Democratic
Florida counties—Miami-Dade, Broward, Volusia, and Palm Beach.[29]
Over the next month the Gore and Bush campaigns would contest the
manual recounts in both state and federal courts, with the Bush campaign
trying to get the recounts stopped and the Gore campaign pushing for
them to go forward. The Florida secretary of state, Katherine Harris,
a Republican, was also involved in the recount, because it was her job
to certify the election results, and how to count the recounted ballots
played into the certification. The initial date to certify the election results
was November 18; the Florida Supreme Court, which had a majority
of Democratic justices, extended that deadline by six days to allow the
inclusion of recounted ballots. On November 26 Harris certified Bush the
winner of Florida's presidential election, with a vote margin of 537 votes.

Throughout the on again, off again recounts, Bush never relinquished
his lead in votes. Eventually, the Florida State Supreme Court ordered a
statewide manual recount of the ballots with undervotes (those famous
hanging, dimpled, or pregnant chads), but the U.S. Supreme Court, the
evening of December 12, in a 5-to-4 decision (*Bush* v. *Gore*), ordered
the statewide recount stopped. The state's electors had to be certified by
December 12 to prevent a potential congressional challenge to the electors. The Supreme Court decision, while citing problems with the vote

counting in Florida in 2000, ruled that there was not enough time to complete the statewide recount before the December 12 deadline. With the recount stopped and Bush still ahead, Florida's twenty-five electoral votes went to Bush, and the 2000 election was finally decided.[30]

Following the election the *Washington Post* and other news organizations commissioned a study to examine 175,010 ballots in all sixty-seven counties in Florida, ballots that contained either undervotes, with no discernible vote for president, or overvotes, with more than one vote for president. The study concludes that if the recounts—which were stopped first by state election officials and then by the U.S. Supreme Court—had gone forward, Bush likely still would have had more votes than Gore, by a margin somewhere between 225 and 493 votes, depending on the standards for counting the ballots.[31]

However, the study also suggests that, if there had been a full statewide recount, Gore might have narrowly won the state but by less than 200 votes. The study looked only at ballots not included in the machine count; it did not include the disputed butterfly ballots in Palm Beach County. The study finds that the real loss of votes for Gore was not in the undervotes or overvotes but in the votes cast on butterfly ballots in Palm Beach County and the two-page presidential ballot in Duval County. The study estimates that, between the two counties, Gore lost approximately 15,000 votes.

Despite the outcome of the presidential election in Florida, there was no serious consideration given to reforming or eliminating the Electoral College. The system has worked surprisingly well since the country's founding and continues to be the foundation for presidential elections in the United States. As a result, candidates will continue to develop strategies to get to 270 Electoral College votes.

CONCLUSION

Changes in the general election between 1968 and 2008 saw more focused strategies on how to reach 270 Electoral College votes. While this means some of the most populous states received little if any attention from presidential candidates, it also means that some smaller states received attention they would not otherwise have received. In 2008 the Obama campaign expanded the number of states in play to include states that had not in recent elections voted for Democratic candidates, in part by expanding the electorate in those states. The period between 1968 and 2008 saw both the return and the institutionalization of general election debates, ensuring that interested Americans across the country could see the candidates answering questions on issues facing the country. Even the 2000 presidential election, which was eventually ended by the nine justices on the Supreme Court, led to changes in election administration, which moved toward fairer and more accurate elections.

CHAPTER FIVE

THE ROLE OF TECHNOLOGY

THE PERIOD BETWEEN 1968 AND 2008 saw an expansion of the opportunities for Americans to engage in the political process, first with the growth of television from just three networks to a vast array of cable channels and then with the development of the Internet.

CABLE TELEVISION

The number of American households subscribing to cable television grew from 16 million in the late 1970s to more than 65 million in the late 1990s.[1] In 1979 C-SPAN was created, to provide coverage of the House of Representatives and other public affairs programming. In 1986 C-SPAN2 was created, to expand coverage to the U.S. Senate, and a third C-SPAN channel, C-SPAN3, was created in 2001. In 1980 Cable News Network (CNN), became the first twenty-four-hour news network. Darrell West describes the changes in television news that occurred in the 1980s and 1990s. "The clubby world of ABC, CBS, NBC and PBS gave way to nearly one hundred television channels. All news channels such as CNN, MSNBC, and CNBC offered political coverage around the clock, whether or not there was breaking news. New television networks appeared, such as Fox, UPN, and WB. . . . Local news stations moved aggressively into coverage of national political events."[2]

With the growth of cable television the outlets for coverage of campaigns, politics, and public affairs increased exponentially. American viewers had a wide variety of sources for information about candidates and campaigns, and almost any point of view could be found on some

73

cable channel. Similarly, candidates had more options to present their ideas to the American public.

More cable channels also meant more demand for content to fill those hours, which sometimes works to the detriment of candidates. For example, when Howard Dean addressed his supporters following his third-place finish in the Iowa caucuses in 2004, he declared to a cheering crowd, "Not only are we going to New Hampshire, but we're going to South Carolina, and Oklahoma, and Arizona, and North Dakota, and New Mexico. We're going to California, and Texas, and New York. We're going to South Dakota, and Oregon, and Washington, and Michigan, and then we're going to Washington, D.C., to take back the White House. Yeah!"[3] While the speech fired up his supporters in the room, it made Dean look slightly crazy when played on television, and it played over and over on television, particularly on cable television, between the Iowa caucus and the New Hampshire primary.

TECHNOLOGICAL INNOVATION BY THE
NATIONAL PARTY COMMITTEES

The Republican National Committee led the way with technological innovation. Following the Watergate scandal in the early 1970s, President Nixon's resignation in 1974 as a result of the scandal, and President Ford's loss to Jimmy Carter in 1976, the Republican Party was in disarray. When William Brock took over as RNC chair in 1977, he was determined to rebuild the party at the national level. Brock embarked on an ambitious, and ultimately successful, campaign to develop a direct mail fundraising program. During his four-year tenure as chair of the RNC Brock increased the number of direct mail contributors to the RNC from 350,000 to 1.2 million.[4] During the 1977–78 election cycle the RNC raised $25 million in direct mail; in the 1979–80 cycle that number more than doubled, to $54 million.[5] Moreover, the average direct mail contribution to the party was $29, countering the argument that only wealthy donors were contributing to the party. The direct mail program that Brock established provided the basis for the Republican Party's success in raising hard dollars, which exceeded the hard dollars raised by the Democratic Party for decades. It wasn't until the 2004 election that the

Democratic Party was on a par with the Republican Party in hard money dollars, in large part because of the efforts of Terry McAuliffe.

Following the 2000 presidential election the Democratic National Committee chose long-time Democratic fundraiser Terry McAuliffe to chair the DNC. When he took over, McAuliffe was appalled at the lack of technological sophistication he found at headquarters. "Ten-year-old computers and outdated technology were the norm. . . . The DNC had a database of only seventy thousand e-mail addresses . . . the national party had no voter files to contact potential supporters . . . [in the state party files] there were twenty-seven million wrong addresses and phone numbers."[6] McAuliffe committed to bring the DNC into the twenty-first century with a new headquarters, technological advances across the board, and a more efficient and aggressive fundraising operation. During his tenure as chair of the DNC McAuliffe increased donors to the committee from 400,000 to 2.7 million, increased the committee's e-mail list from 70,000 to 3.8 million, and created a voter file of 178 million registered voters.

THE INTERNET

As television changed political communication during the last half of the twentieth century, the Internet created an explosion of all forms of communication at the beginning of the twenty-first century. Internet usage in campaigns exploded exponentially between 2000 and 2008, and its use in the 2012 election will grow even more.

The Internet before 2000

In *The First Campaign,* Garrett Graff traces the role of the Internet in politics back to 1980.[7] David Hughes, a retired Army officer active in local Colorado politics, created an online bulletin board service and named it "Roger's Bar," after a real bar in Colorado City where Democrats gathered to discuss politics. As Graff describes this early online endeavor, "Hughes went down to the actual namesake pub and convinced the staff to install a telephone jack in one of their booths so that patrons of the bar could log on to his online bulletin board to talk politics using Hughes' laptop and an acoustic modem." Graff describes Hughes's bulletin board as "the first online political endeavor on the then very nascent Internet."

During the 1980s and 1990s there were a few savvy political professionals who recognized the political potential of the Internet; in addition to Hughes, Graff cites Joe Trippi, who later was instrumental in Howard Dean's use of the Internet during the 2004 election, and Karl Rove, the architect of the two George W. Bush campaigns. However, the Internet, when it was used in campaigns at all in the 1980s and 1990s, was often only an electronic bulletin board, not unlike what Hughes created in 1980. Dianne Feinstein, during her U.S. Senate campaign in 1994, was the first candidate to create a candidate website, but "it was little more than an online brochure—with basic information about the candidate, perhaps some issue stances, and maybe a form to print out and mail in with a contribution." While the Internet played a modest role in the 1996 election, "few political campaigns used the Internet, there is no indication of massive use, and there is no evidence of any significant effect on election outcomes."[8] It wasn't until the 2000 presidential election that the Internet's potential became obvious.

The Internet in 2000

The first big technological change in the 2000 election was in fundraising. Candidates began to realize the potential to raise money online. Until the 2000 campaign candidates raised money in three main ways: direct solicitation of potential donors by the candidate or his or her finance committee, fundraising events, and direct mail or telemarketing solicitations. Personal solicitation by the candidate or a finance committee is the most cost effective, but it is time consuming and means that the candidate spends time raising money at the expense of time spent meeting potential voters. Also, because it is time consuming, most personal solicitation by the candidate focuses on wealthy donors—those who have the ability to write, in presidential elections, checks of $1,000 or more. Fundraising events are costly and time consuming for the campaign, and direct mail and telemarketing require considerable lead time to be successful. All three techniques place much of the onus on the campaign. Campaigns need to construct lists of potential donors and then reach out to those donors.

With online fundraising, donors can reach out to campaigns to contribute; they do not have to wait for campaigns to come to them. They can go to the candidate's website and make a donation with a credit card. Online fundraising is particularly effective with donors who wish to make small donations. Soliciting small donors is unrealistic for candidate solicitation and even for most fundraising events; the returns in donations aren't worth the fundraising costs. With online fundraising, seeking small donations is much more realistic; the only costs to the campaigns are establishing a secure website and processing credit cards. John Emerson, Gary Hart's California campaign manager during Hart's 1984 presidential campaign, describes the difference in the fundraising process before and after online fundraising. In 1984 donors who wanted to contribute to a campaign had to find the campaign's address, get a stamp, write a check, and mail it in, and then the campaign had to deposit the check. Commented Emerson, "Can you imagine how much more [money] there would have been if all they [donors] had to do was go to a Gary Hart website?"[9]

During the 2000 primary election John McCain won the New Hampshire Republican primary February 1, defeating George W. Bush, the front-runner. In the ten days following the primary, McCain raised $2.2 million online.[10] By Super Tuesday, on March 7, almost 40 percent of McCain's $10 million had been raised online. His webmaster boasted that at times the McCain campaign received $30,000 an hour.[11] The McCain campaign also experimented with other ways to use the Internet. They enlisted online volunteers to download phone bank lists to reach voters at no cost, as opposed to paying large sums of money to employ professional phone banks. Campaign literature was available to print out and distribute, again at virtually no cost to the campaign. In stark contrast, the official Bush campaign website offered little more than links to speech transcripts, position papers, and press releases. Later the campaign did experiment with e-mail communications and received an average of $200,000 to $300,000 per e-mail, but it still paled in comparison to McCain's extensive Internet campaign efforts.[12]

Al Gore proved to have a slightly more effective online presence than did Bush in the 2000 election. The Gore campaign sent e-mails to its supporters asking them to forward virtual postcards to their friends, and the campaign was able to raise hundreds of thousands of dollars a day at its peak.

The Internet in 2004

The 2004 campaign saw not only continued online fundraising but also the use of the Internet for organizing supporters. The Howard Dean presidential campaign did both. Joe Trippi, the Dean campaign manager, recognized the implications the Internet could have for the campaign during the spring of 2003. The power of Internet fundraising was first apparent in the days preceding and following the announcement of Dean's candidacy. Despite what the Washington press corps considered a disastrous appearance by Dean on *Meet the Press* the day before the official announcement of his campaign, Dean raised almost $100,000 online that day. The day of his official announcement, June 23, he raised another $200,000 online. The money continued to pour into the Dean campaign in the final days of June.

Seeing the money flow in, Trippi posted on the campaign's website a challenge to Dean's supporters to raise $6.5 million by June 30, the end of the second-quarter FEC reporting period. A characterization of a baseball bat was posted on the website, and the bat "filled in" as contributions came in. Garrett Graff, who was working on the Dean campaign at the time, describes the success of the baseball bat fundraising ploy as follows: "That Monday, June 30, the spigot just opened. Every half hour Nicco [Mele, Dean's webmaster] posted updates and let the bat fill in a little more. . . . By the time the clock struck midnight and Nicco posted the final update to the bat, more than seventy-three thousand people had contributed $7.6 million to Howard Dean in the second quarter, with an average contribution of $112."[13]

The baseball bat gimmick was so successful that the campaign continued to tie online fundraising to real-world political events. For example, in July 2003 the campaign organized around a Republican Party $2,000-a-plate fundraising luncheon, organized by Dick Cheney, challenging its supporters to raise more money than the Republican luncheon. The campaign raised twice as much money as the luncheon—$500,000, compared to $250,000 for the Republicans—and had almost tenfold the number of contributors. One hundred and twenty five people attended the luncheon, while 9,700 people contributed to the Dean campaign's challenge.[14] In the end, the Dean campaign illustrated the power of the Internet to raise small donations and became the precursor to the Obama campaign's Internet fundraising four years later. Almost 60 percent of Dean's campaign contributions were in donations of $200 or less, compared to just 7 percent in donations of $2,000 or more.[15]

The other major online initiative of the Dean campaign in 2004 was online organizing. In 1998, during the impeachment proceedings against President Bill Clinton, an organization called MoveOn.org was formed by two California Silicon Valley entrepreneurs. They invited people to sign an online petition to "Censure President Clinton and Move On to Pressing Issues Facing the Nation."[16] Hundreds of thousands of individuals signed up. In June 2003 MoveOn.org decided to engage in the 2004 presidential campaign.[17] Just days before his official campaign announcement, Howard Dean sent a letter to MoveOn.org members asking them to support his campaign.[18] Just after Dean's announcement MoveOn.org conducted an online "vote" of its members to ascertain their support for the various Democratic candidates seeking the nomination and to see if any candidate had enough support to warrant an endorsement (the organization said it would endorse a candidate who received more than 50 percent of the vote in the online election). Over 300,000 MoveOn.org members participated in the vote. While no candidate received 50 percent of the vote, Howard Dean far and away had the most support. Almost 44 percent of MoveOn.org's members supported Dean; the only two other candidates with double-digit support were far behind, with almost 24 percent of MoveOn.org's members supporting Dennis Kucinich and almost 16 percent supporting John Kerry.[19]

While MoveOn.org did not endorse the Dean campaign, the campaign was clearly helped by the online organizational presence MoveOn.org had developed. The Dean campaign also took advantage of meetups. Meetup.com is an organization started in 2002 that brings people of common interests together. On his first day on the campaign in January 2003 Joe Trippi ordered that a link to Meetup.com be put on the Dean campaign website.[20] Trippi had noticed that there were more Dean supporters who wanted to meet up—432 across the country—than there were for any other Democratic candidate in the race. After the link to Meetup.com was placed on the Dean website, that number jumped to 2,700. By the end of the campaign there were almost 200,000 Dean campaign Meetup.com members. The power of the Dean meetups is best described by a meetup in New York City in March 2003. Initially 50–60 people signed up to attend the meetup, but by Monday, two days before the meetup, 300 hundred people had signed up. When Trippi realized that Dean would be in New York the day of the meetup, he suggested that Dean stop by. When the Dean campaign e-mailed its supporters to say that Dean was going to try to attend the meetup, the number signed up jumped to 500. In the end, there were 500 Dean supporters in the room and another 300 to 400 outside on the sidewalk.

The Dean for America Meetup.com groups met the first Wednesday of every month, and Dean, after his experience at the March New York City meetup, tried to stop by the meetup in whatever city he was in. Garrett Graff describes how the Dean meetups grew:

> Ordinary citizens stepped up to lead their meetup since the national campaign organization could never hope to staff so many events (by the end of the campaign there were approximately 2,000 Dean for America meetups around the country). In the campaign head-quarters a team worked almost around the clock to provide the letter writing supplies, campaign stickers, and resources that the groups demanded. . . . It was a new model for politics: people not waiting for leadership but instead taking the initiative for change and organizing themselves.[21]

These interpersonal groups became a precursor to the online social networking sites that would play such a prominent role in the 2008 election, especially for the Obama campaign.

The Dean campaign also took advantage of the relatively new phenomenon of blogging. While the earliest blogs date back to the mid-1990s, blogs became part of the political landscape early in 2002. The Dean campaign used blogs to complement their meetups. Michael Cornfield describes one example of this:

> In 2003, the Dean campaign posted 2,910 entries on its Blog for America and received 314,121 comments, which were also posted there. As the result of one of these comments, 115,632 handwritten letters were sent from supporters to eligible voters in the upcoming Iowa caucuses and New Hampshire primary. (Meetup captains were issued lists, stamped envelopes, and a sample text for the letter writers to follow.)[22]

The Dean campaign used the Internet to draw supporters into the campaign and allowed them to become a part of the campaign in ways that had not happened previously. The campaign encouraged supporters to interact with the campaign; no longer was there the top-down organizational structure that had characterized presidential campaigns in the past.

The 2004 presidential election also saw the use of the Internet to present campaign-related media independent of the two candidates' campaigns. One of the most popular and most watched was produced by Jib-Jab, a digital entertainment studio founded in 1999 by Evan and Gregg Spiridellis. During the 2004 campaign the brothers created a flash video satirizing George W. Bush and John Kerry. The video featured animated caricatures of Bush and Kerry set to the tune of "This Land Is Your Land." The video immediately went viral; at one point it got more than a million hits in twenty-four hours.[23]

The Internet in 2008

By the 2008 presidential election the interactive relationship between a campaign and its supporters exemplified by the Dean campaign became full blown in the Obama campaign. As Alan Rosenblatt observes, "In a world where the power of the people is enabled by digital and mobile networks, campaigns have to adjust how they view their supporters. Rather than viewing them as message receptacles and followers to organize, campaigns have to treat supporters as strategic partners."[24] The former describes the relationship between campaigns and their supporters as late as the 2000 presidential election; by 2008 the Obama campaign began to see its supporters as strategic partners, and technology played a key part in that. Even before Obama made the commitment to run, his campaign decided that, if he did run, "technology . . . would be at the core of our campaign from the start. . . . We decided to green-light the building of a website, heavy on video and tools for our supporters to organize and raise money and have discussions and find each other—our own social networking site."[25] The social networking site the campaign created was MyBarackObama.com, or MyBO, as it became known.

By 2008 almost half of all Americans were using the Internet for political purposes. A survey conducted by the Pew Research Center for the People and the Press found that "46% of all adults used the Internet to get news about the campaigns, share their views, and mobilize others."[26] Moreover, the study finds that almost a third of all Americans (29 percent) used the Internet to follow campaigns, unfettered by the filter of news organizations or campaigns. These Americans were getting information about campaigns from primary sources such as debates and speeches. E-mail was the predominant tool for online conversations—a third of e-mail users received campaign information at least once a week—but the study found that text messaging was beginning to play a role in political interaction; almost 10 percent of those who used text messaging sent or received texts related to politics. The study found that 35 percent of adults had watched some type of political video online, and 10 percent had used social networking sites for political activity. While most online social networking sites were in their infancy or didn't exist at all during the 2004 presidential campaign, by the 2008 election social networks were a firm part of American culture. Facebook alone, which was founded in early 2004, had 36 million users in the United States by mid-2008. The Obama campaign took advantage of the prevalence of social networks with MyBarackObama.com. Julie Barko Germany, the director of the Institute for Politics, Democracy, and the Internet at George Washington University, describes MyBO as a way "to use the Internet to recreate as much as possible offline relationships in the online world by allowing members to meet each other, build relationships, and attend and hold local meetings and events."[27] In other words, to do online what the Dean campaign had done offline with its meetups.

MyBarackObama.com was a way for Obama supporters to participate in the campaign as "strategic partners," as Alan Rosenblatt called them, either through organizing their friends, raising money, or most important, voting. Joe Rospars, the Obama campaign's new media director, describes the campaign's strategic thinking vis-à-vis its supporters:

> We've tried to bring two principles to this campaign. One is lowering the barriers to entry and making it as easy as possible for folks who come to our Web site. The other is raising the expectation of what it means to be a supporter. It's not enough to have a bumper sticker. We want you to give five dollars, make some calls, host an event. If you look at the messages we send to people over time, there's a presumption that they will organize.[28]

MyBarackObama enabled supporters to register to vote, start a listserv, download an Obama news widget, make calls to their friends (in September 2008 the campaign introduced an iPhone application that sorted friends' phone numbers by key battleground states), receive text message updates from the campaign, and create their own fundraising page, complete with a personal fundraising thermometer that rose as personal contacts contributed to the campaign.[29] All these opportunities engaged supporters in the campaign. At the same time, as supporters interacted with the campaign, the campaign used that information to refine its approach to its supporters. Rospars explains that "each time a supporter interacts with the campaign . . . data specialists create new layers for targeting that person by region, engagement, and volunteer preferences."[30]

The Obama campaign also used videos to communicate with their supporters. Typically the videos came from David Plouffe, the campaign manager, and outlined the campaign's strategy. Plouffe describes one such video:

> I wanted to pick one state to demonstrate why our supporters' dedication and assistance was so sorely needed, and why, if they let up at all, we would lose. For this exercise I chose Florida, and we laid it all out in the video—our statewide budget ($38 million), where we were spending it by category, and how we thought we'd win the state. I covered everything, from turnout and registration to persuasion numbers and targets.[31]

The video demonstrates the way the Obama campaign sought to bring its supporters into the campaign in ways that hadn't been done in previous campaigns and in a way that new technology permitted. Plouffe commented that "this video message was one of the most effective ones we sent; the response factors we could measure—contributions, spike in volunteer hours—unmistakably bore this out. . . . People felt like they were being leveled with, that we were explaining clearly how their time and money was being utilized. And they felt that we valued and needed them."[32]

Just as the JibJab "This Land" video caught the attention of potential voters in 2004, another video independent of the two campaigns received widespread attention in 2008. A political action group called the Jewish Council for Education and Research enlisted Comedy Central comedienne Sarah Silverman to make a video to encourage young Jews to reach out to their grandparents and encourage them to vote for Barack Obama. Titled "The Great Schlep," the video encourages young Jews to visit, or if a visit wasn't possible, to call or e-mail their grandparents to persuade them to support Obama.[33] The video had 7 million hits, and 13,000 people committed to calling or visiting elderly relatives in Florida.[34] Earlier in the year recording artist will.i.am released a music video setting to music Barack Obama's New Hampshire concession speech. The video, titled "Yes We Can," had more than 4 million YouTube views in the first week it was released and 15 million views during the course of the election.[35]

In addition to social networking sites, social media sites also gave potential voters new opportunities to engage in the presidential campaign. YouTube did not exist during the 2004 presidential campaign, but by 2008 anyone with a cell phone was able to take pictures and post them on the web. While this empowered citizens to be active participants in the images of political campaigns, it also meant everything a campaign or a candidate did was open for public scrutiny. The role YouTube might play in presidential politics was foreshadowed in 2006, when Virginia Senator George Allen, considered a possible Republican presidential candidate in 2008, made an insulting remark about a videographer for his opponent's campaign who was taping Allen's public events. Allen referred to the videographer, a young man born and raised in Virginia but of Indian descent, as "macaca," a term that in some cultures is considered an ethnic slur.[36] The Allen campaign never recovered from the comment, and Allen lost his reelection to James Webb and with it any chance of getting the Republican presidential nomination in 2008.[37]

The Obama campaign had a painful example of the role that instant communication could play during the primary campaign, when at a private fundraiser in San Francisco just weeks before the Pennsylvania primary he described residents of small towns in Pennsylvania (and the Midwest) as "bitter" and "cling[ing] to guns or religion or antipathy to people who aren't like them or anti-immigrant or anti-trade sentiment as a way to explain their frustrations."[38] A woman attending the fundraiser recorded the comments and posted them on the Huffington Post website.

During the 2008 campaign YouTube became an instant source of video material about the campaigns. David Plouffe, in talking about Barack Obama's speech on race in Philadelphia in March 2008, said, "Most people did not watch the speech on TV. It was delivered on a Tuesday morning, when most people were at work. Instead, people watched it online, most of them on YouTube, either as it was happening or at their leisure later that day or in the days to come."[39] While YouTube could be helpful to campaigns in getting their messages out, it also could be detrimental. Perhaps there was no better example of the destructive nature of instant video than the videos of the Reverend Jeremiah Wright's inflammatory remarks weeks before Obama's Philadelphia speech. Wright was the pastor at the church in Chicago the Obamas attended, he had officiated at their marriage, and he had baptized their daughters. While Obama eventually disassociated himself from Wright, the sermons flooding the cable networks and the Internet in March 2008 caused great consternation to the Obama campaign and provided the impetus for the Philadelphia speech.

Steve Grubbs, the Iowa campaign manager for former Wisconsin governor and 2008 Republican presidential candidate Tommy Thompson, described the role of YouTube in the 2008 presidential election: "The thing I thought really changed in this presidential cycle more than any other cycle was how quickly YouTube could make you famous or infamous."[40] Illustrating Grubbs's point, McCain campaign manager Rick Davis noted at a postelection conference that Sarah Palin "had 75 percent name ID in a week."[41]

The democratization of presidential elections through newfound technologies extended to presidential debates. While the Commission on Presidential Debates had begun using town hall forums for debates in 1992, those town halls allowed only undecided voters in the city where the debate was being held to participate. In 2007 YouTube partnered with CNN to sponsor two presidential debates, one for Democratic candidates in July 2007 and a second for Republican candidates in November. No longer were debate questions solely the purview of journalists or those citizens able to physically attend the debate; citizens were able to submit video questions for the candidates to answer.

CONCLUSION

The technological changes that preceded the 2000, 2004, and 2008 presidential elections increased the democratization of the relationship between campaigns, supporters, and potential voters. In 2000, with just a few mouse clicks, supporters could contribute money to campaigns. By 2004 not only did Internet fundraising soar but so did online organizing.

By 2008 the Obama campaign, through its MyBarackObama.com social networking site, was able to engage voters in the campaign in a variety of ways, and on the voters' terms, and also expected them to be engaged. In addition, social media sites such as MySpace and Facebook enabled citizens to connect with each other and with the campaigns. YouTube created a medium for images of the campaigns to be instantly shared by campaign supporters, by opponents, and by organizations independent of the campaigns and even presented a venue for citizens nationwide to ask questions in presidential debates.

CHAPTER SIX

CHANGES IN ELECTION LAWS

THE FORTY-YEAR PERIOD BETWEEN 1968 and 2008 saw changes in election laws in the United States—changes that ended discriminatory practices, expanded the eligible voting population, made it easier for citizens to register and vote, and addressed problems with election administration in states and localities.

ENDING DISCRIMINATORY PRACTICES

The first changes in election laws were aimed to end discriminatory practices that disenfranchised minorities, particularly African Americans, during more than half of the twentieth century. Despite being guaranteed the right to vote by the passage of the Fifteenth Amendment to the U.S. Constitution in 1870, by the early 1900s provisions had been put in place, particularly in southern states, that in practice disenfranchised African Americans. Among these practices were poll taxes, which required the payment of a tax before voting, and literacy tests, which allowed state officials to test the literacy of citizens before allowing them to vote. Both of these practices disproportionately affected African Americans, who were both more likely to be poor, and thus unable to pay the poll tax, and less likely to have high levels of literacy, because of discrimination in education.[1]

Poll taxes were eliminated in 1964, with the ratification of the Twenty-Fourth Amendment to the Constitution, the amendment that prohibits states from tying the right to vote in federal elections to payment of a poll tax. At the time the amendment was ratified five states—Virginia,

Alabama, Arkansas, Mississippi, and Texas—still had poll taxes. In 1996 the Supreme Court, in *Harper* v. *Virginia Board of Elections,* declared poll taxes a violation of the Equal Protection Clause of the Fourteenth Amendment, and poll taxes were eliminated in state elections as well as federal elections.

Literacy tests subsided in the South after the passage of the Voting Rights Act of 1965. The act took the process of registering voters out of the hands of state officials and placed it into the hands of federal officials. Federal officials were less likely to engage in discriminatory practices, and as a result the practice of administering literacy tests was suspended in much of the South. Literacy tests were formally abolished with the passage of the Voting Rights Act of 1970. To ensure that discriminatory practices ceased the Voting Rights Act of 1965 also required states with a history of discrimination to submit any changes in voting procedures to the Department of Justice, a provision referred to as preclearance. That provision was to expire in 2006, but in 2006 Congress voted to extend it for another twenty-five years.

EXPANDING THE ELIGIBLE VOTING POPULATION

A voting age of twenty-one had been the law of the United States since the country's founding. While proposals to lower the voting age to eighteen arose after every major war—with the argument that if men were old enough to fight they should be able to vote—the proposals were not seriously considered until the Vietnam War.[2] As the Vietnam War raged in the 1960s there was increasing pressure on the states and the federal government to lower the voting age from twenty-one to eighteen. At the time there was a mandatory draft in the United States, and many young men (only men were eligible to be drafted) who opposed the war had no voice in elections to influence U.S. policy toward the war. The phrase "old enough to fight, old enough to vote" became a rallying cry for those in favor of lowering the voting age, and numerous interest groups formed to lobby for a lower voting age.

An amendment to the Voting Rights Act of 1970 to reduce the voting age to eighteen passed the Senate in the spring of 1970, and the House reluctantly went along.[3] President Nixon signed the legislation, though he questioned the constitutionality of Congress changing the voting age. In late 1970 the Supreme Court, in *Oregon v. Mitchell*, concluded that Congress had the power to change the voting age for federal, but not state, elections.[4] To avoid the logistical problems that different voting ages in state and federal elections would cause, Congress approved a constitutional amendment lowering the voting age to eighteen in both state and federal elections, and in 1971 the Twenty-Sixth Amendment to the Constitution was ratified, extending voting rights to eighteen-to-twenty-year-olds.[5]

LIBERALIZING ELECTION LAWS

The first effort to liberalize election laws in the period between 1968 and 2008 occurred in 1970. Before 1970 most states in the United States had lengthy residential requirements, requiring citizens to live in their states as long as a year before they could vote in elections. As the United States became a more mobile society, residency requirements became burdensome to more and more citizens. Estimates were that the laws meant that 15 million people were unable to vote in the 1964 elections.[6] The Voting Rights Act of 1970, in addition to abolishing literacy tests, imposed a maximum thirty-day residency in a state as a requirement for voting in a presidential election; in 1972 the U.S. Supreme Court, in *Dunn v. Blumstein,* extended that maximum residency to voting in state and local elections.

The Voting Rights Act of 1970 also imposed a maximum thirty-day closing date for registration for voting in presidential elections. The greater the distance between a state's registration closing date and Election Day, the less likely citizens will register before the deadline, because they simply aren't paying attention until closer to the election. Between 1970 and 2008 many states enacted provisions to shrink the time between registration closing dates and Election Day; by 2008 less than half the states had a thirty-day registration closing date.

Election Day Registration

One characteristic of voting in the United States is that it is a two-step process: citizens must register to vote before they can actually vote, must register before state-imposed deadlines, as discussed above, and if they move from one jurisdiction to another, must reregister to vote in their new jurisdiction. In the 1970s there began the first in a series of changes in election laws to ease the logistical requirements of registration and voting.

Between 1973 and 1976 three states—Maine, Minnesota, and Wisconsin—instituted Election Day registration. Election Day registration still requires a two-step process—citizens still have to both register to vote and then to vote—but they can do both on Election Day and in one place. (North Dakota eliminated registration requirements entirely in 1951; it is the only state that does not require voters to register before they can cast a ballot.) Between 1996 and 2008 the number of states with Election Day registration expanded. By the 2010 midterm elections one-fifth of the states had some form of Election Day registration. In addition to Maine, Minnesota, and Wisconsin, voters could register on election day in Idaho, Iowa, Montana, New Hampshire, Wyoming, and Washington, D.C. Connecticut and Alaska allow Election Day registration but only in presidential elections. Ohio and North Carolina, while not allowing registration on Election Day itself, allow citizens to register to vote at early-voting sites. For example, in North Carolina, same-day registration is permissible three to nineteen days before the actual election.[7]

Allowing citizens to register and vote on the same day removes the two-stage process of first registering to vote and then, later, voting and enables citizens to register when they are most paying attention to elections. Turnout in states with Election Day registration is approximately 7 percent higher than in states without it.[8] In the 2008 presidential election turnout was 6.6 percent higher in states with Election Day registration.[9]

Convenience Voting

Elections in the United States almost always occur on Tuesdays, a work day for most Americans. While states try to set voting hours to accommodate work schedules, the necessity to fit voting into an already full day can pose challenges to Americans. Beginning in the 1980s, to address the difficulties posed by having to vote on just one day, during certain hours, states began to experiment with what became known as convenience voting.

Convenience voting is described as "relaxed administrative rules and procedures by which citizens can cast a ballot at a time and place other than the precinct on Election Day."[10] Convenience voting typically refers to three types of voting—no-excuse absentee voting, early voting, and voting by mail. The argument for convenience voting is that such voting systems will increase turnout in elections, because they allow voters to cast their ballots in ways convenient to the voter. Convenience voting removes the requirement of having to vote on one day, in one location, in a manner that may interfere with work or other personal responsibilities. Voters can fill out their ballots at their leisure in their homes and then mail in the ballots, or they can vote at a day and time convenient to them.

—No-excuse absentee voting: States have long allowed voters who would be out of the state on election day, are unable to vote in person for health reasons, or who had some other state-approved reason for not being able to vote on election day to vote by absentee ballot. However, beginning in the 1980s, more and more states began to allow no-excuse absentee voting, meaning registered voters could vote absentee for any reason. In 2010 thirty states and the District of Columbia offered no-excuse absentee voting.[11] Eight states and the District of Columbia also allow permanent no-excuse absentee voting, meaning that voters can request to automatically receive absentee ballots in future elections.

—Early voting: In the 1980s states also began to experiment with early voting, allowing voters to cast ballots at election offices before Election Day. Texas was one of the first states to allow such early voting.[12] Early voting allows voters to vote at designated early-voting centers before election day. In some states early voting begins as early as late September. By 2010 thirty-two states and the District of Columbia had provisions for early voting.[13]

—Election Day vote centers: Election Day vote centers are located in major population centers, as opposed to the traditional precinct-based election locations. The argument behind Election Day vote centers is that they are convenient to where people work, thus making it easier to vote on Election Day, either on their way to and from work or during lunchtime. Voters are able to vote at any vote center in the county, rather than at a precinct location based on their residence. Larimer County in Colorado first experimented with Election Day vote centers in 2003; by 2008 twenty-one counties in Colorado allowed voting in Election Day vote centers, and some counties in Texas, Indiana, and Tennessee also experimented with Election Day vote centers.[14]

—Vote by mail: Another type of convenience voting is voting by mail. Two states have only vote-by-mail systems. Oregon began experimenting with all-mail elections in state and local elections in the 1980s. In 1995 Senator Bob Packwood resigned his Senate seat, and Oregon used mail ballots in the primary and general special elections to fill Packwood's seat. A subsequent ballot measure enacted in 1998 allows all elections to be conducted entirely by mail, and vote by mail has been the practice in Oregon since 1998. Ballots are mailed to registered voters approximately three weeks before the election, and the voter has three weeks to fill out the ballot and either mail it in or drop it off at a designated site for collection of ballots.[15] In the 2006 elections in Washington State 85 percent of voters voted using no-excuse absentee voting, and in some counties 100 percent of votes were cast that way, creating an essentially vote-by-mail system. In 2008 Washington moved to a vote-by-mail system only.[16]

Research on convenience voting suggests that, while some methods of convenience voting do increase turnout, other methods have no effect on turnout and in some cases may actually decrease turnout. Election Day registration increases turnout, as seen above; most studies find Election Day registration increases turnout by somewhere between 5 and 9 percent.[17] Turnout is also higher in the vote-by-mail states of Oregon and Washington.

However, studies consistently find that early voting only makes it easier for those voters already likely to vote to cast their ballots; very few new voters are brought to the polls by early-vote systems.[18] One study of early voting in the 2008 election concludes, "Early voting is not bringing new voters into the electorate. Instead, it serves more as a convenience for those already likely to vote. Remove early voting, and most (if not all) of those early voters would simply show up on Election Day."[19] The same study finds that, in 2008, in states that had early voting and allowed same-day registration at early-voting sites, 27 percent of voters were new voters. While the authors of the study argue that "only" 27 percent of the voters were new voters, a one quarter increase in the voting roles, particularly over time, can substantially increase turnout in presidential elections. Early voting and no-excuse absentee voting also have been found to increase the accuracy of vote counts, an important consequence for election outcomes.[20]

Registration Reform

Election Day registration was introduced in the 1970s and expanded in the 1990s and 2000s. Efforts to ease registration procedures began in the 1980s, with various registration reform bills introduced in Congress.

Academic studies had long found that one of the major barriers to voting is the requirement that citizens first register to vote and that turnout among registered voters is substantially higher than turnout among the eligible electorate.[21] In 2008, for example, only 63 percent of American adults voted, while the turnout among those registered was nearly 90 percent.[22]

Registration laws also disproportionately discourage minorities and those with limited incomes—those who are least able to navigate the registration procedures.[23] A report of the United States Commission on Civil Rights, ten years after the enactment of the Voting Rights Act of 1965, states that

> While formal barriers [to registration] no longer exist, the lack of interest and of affirmative attempts to register voters on the part of county registrars become hindrances to participation. These hindrances include restrictive time and location for registration, the inadequate number of minority registration personnel, and purging of the registration rolls and reregistration. . . . Minority registration still lags behind that of whites, in some cases far behind. Any hindrance which makes it harder to register ensures that the gap will persist.[24]

The theory behind easing registration laws is that if people were able to register to vote as they went about their daily lives, rather than in specific registration offices, registration would increase and, therefore, so would turnout. As discussed above, one of the barriers to larger turnout in the United States is the requirement that potential voters must register to vote before they can vote and must reregister each time they move from one residence to another. The National Voter Registration Act of 1993 was one effort to address this problem, by expanding the opportunities for American citizens to register and to make registration a part of ongoing interactions with government agencies.

In 1993 President Clinton, as one of his early acts as president, signed into law the National Voter Registration Act of 1993, commonly known as the motor voter law. The National Voter Registration Act (NVRA) allows for registration in motor vehicle offices and social service offices. In an increasingly mobile society people move often, and movement often requires acquiring a new driver's license or car registration. Many people move over the summer, and registration deadlines, in states that have them, are in October. Enabling someone to register to vote when he or she applies for a driver's license or car registration, presumably shortly after a move, captures people who move over the summer but don't realize they need to register at their new residence until the state registration deadline has passed. Among those registered in 2008, almost one quarter (21 percent) report having registered at a DMV office.

Yet the evidence of whether motor voter registration has increased registration and turnout, as it was intended to do, is mixed. Turnout in 1996 and 2000, the first two presidential elections after motor voter took effect, was not significantly higher than in 1992.[25] Yet one study, looking at the effects of motor voter on registration and voting fifteen years after the enactment of the legislation, finds that the NVRA increased registration by approximately 3 percent and increased turnout in presidential years, but not off years, by 3.5 percent.[26]

REFORMING ELECTION ADMINISTRATION

The 2000 presidential election and the protracted battle for Florida's twenty-five electoral votes illustrates the problems with the administration of elections in the United States. Voting machines were outdated and unreliable, and registration rolls were inaccurate. As a result of the election administration deficiencies that occurred in the 2000 presidential election, Congress passed the Help America Vote Act (HAVA) in 2002. HAVA mandates that states replace the punch-card voting systems and lever voting systems. It was the punch-card machines that used chads that caused so many problems with the vote count in Florida in 2000. HAVA also requires all states to develop computerized statewide voter registration lists. Before HAVA many states maintained registration lists at the local level, and often they were not computerized. In Maine, for example, registration lists were kept in registrar's offices in 517 different towns, and in some of those towns the registrar's office was only open on the first Tuesday of the month from 2 to 3 o'clock.[27]

HAVA also requires states to provide provisional ballots to anyone who shows up at the polls to vote and claims to be a registered voter. A provisional ballot allows a voter to cast a ballot even if he or she is not on the registration rolls. The voter's registration is then verified, and if he or she is indeed an eligible voter, the ballot is counted. Before HAVA the rules for the use of provisional ballots varied among the states. Seventeen states allowed for provisional ballots, five states allowed for affidavit ballots, and four had provisional ballots to be used in very limited circumstances. Overall, eighteen states did not have any form of provisional ballot before passage of HAVA.[28] This meant that if the registration rolls were incorrect and the voter was incorrectly left off the rolls the voter had no recourse and no means to vote. In the 2008 elections, one in forty Americans who voted cast a provisional ballot.[29] HAVA also created a new federal agency, the Election Assistance Commission, to administer HAVA, to provide assistance to states in improving voting technologies, and to monitor state compliance.

As stated above, HAVA mandates that states replace punch-card and lever voting systems. Initially these systems were thought to be best replaced by electronic voting machines (technically known as direct recording electronic voting systems, or DRE machines). However, concerns were soon raised about the lack of any paper record of votes if the machines broke down or if a recount became necessary, and there began a demand for machines with a voter-verified paper audit trail. By the 2008 election there were a variety of voting machines in use in the United States. The most commonly used machine was the DRE without a paper trail; the Election Assistance Commission found 281,370 such machines, used in twenty-three states.[30] However, forty-three states used—in at least some areas—an optical scan system, in which a voter filled out a paper ballot that was then optically or digitally scanned.

CONCLUSION

The Voting Rights Acts of 1965 and 1970, along with the Twenty-Fourth Amendment, removes discriminatory voting practices, as does HAVA, with the guarantee of provisional voting. The Twenty-Sixth Amendment expanded the voting age population to include eighteen-to-twenty-year-olds. Motor voter legislation makes it easier to register to vote, and HAVA seeks to make election administration fairer and more uniform across the country.

The changes in election laws between 1968 and 2008 increased the democratization of presidential elections. Discriminatory practices against African Americans, which existed almost since the passage of the Fifteenth Amendment, were removed. More young people were given the right to vote. Both registration and voting became more convenient for voters. Election administration practices were modernized, though the best practices for administering elections continued to evolve.

CHAPTER SEVEN

THE CHANGING ELECTORATE

THE FOUR DECADES BETWEEN 1970 and 2010 saw population shifts in
the United States that had implications for presidential elections. Over
the forty-year period the population of the United States increased by
105 million, from 203 million in 1970 to just over 308 million in 2010.
However, the growth in population was not even throughout the country. Each decade from 1970 to 2010 saw substantial increases in the
population in the southern and western states, while the population in
the Northeast and the Midwest increased much more slowly. In the most
recent decade, between 2000 and 2010, the population in the South grew
14.3 percent and the population in the West grew 13.8 percent, while
the population in the Northeast and the Midwest grew 3.2 percent and
3.9 percent, respectively.[1]

The changes in the population led, each decade, to congressional
reapportionment and, consequently, to changes in the number of Electoral College votes assigned to each state. Between 1970 and 2010 the
South gained twenty-seven Electoral College votes and the West gained
twenty-six. In contrast, the Midwest lost twenty-seven and the Northeast, twenty-five.[2] Following the 2010 census Texas and Florida picked
up the most electoral votes, with Texas gaining four and Florida two. Six
other states, all in the South and West (Arizona, Georgia, Nevada, South
Carolina, Utah, and Washington), picked up one electoral vote each. In
the Northeast and Midwest, Ohio and New York each lost two electoral
votes, and Illinois, Iowa, Massachusetts, Michigan, Missouri, New Jersey, and Pennsylvania each lost one. Louisiana was the only state not in
the Northeast or Midwest to lose an Electoral College vote.

CHANGES IN STATE POPULATIONS

Shifts in the population suggest possibilities for changes in the demographic groups influential in presidential elections. The southern and western states now have higher percentages of African Americans and Latinos than do those in the Northeast and Midwest. The greatest change in the country is the rapidly growing Latino population. Between 1970 and 2008 the Latino population in the United States increased by over 38 million people, from 9.6 million to 48.4 million.[3] Between 2000 and 2010, the increase in the Latino population accounted for more than half of the growth in the U.S. population, and at 16 percent of the total population in the United States, Latinos are the largest minority group in the country.[4]

The 2010 census illustrates the continuing diversity of the American population. The percentage of African Americans increased in every state except Illinois, Michigan, and Hawaii, and the Latino population increased in all states between 2000 and 2010. Table 7-1 looks at changes in the African American, Latino, and Asian populations in the most recent battleground states.

Virginia was a key to Obama's victory in 2008. One-third of Virginia's population is now minority—African American, Latino, or Asian. The African American population increased by almost 12 percent between 2000 and 2010, the Latino population almost doubled, and the Asian population increased by two-thirds. Other battleground states also saw increases in minorities. In Colorado, Latinos compose 20 percent of the population, and in Nevada, over one-quarter of the population is Latino. In the 2008 election African Americans voted overwhelmingly Democratic, and 75 percent of Latinos voted Democratic.[5]

Demographic changes in state populations could also have implications for states currently not considered battleground states. For example, almost half of Texas's population is now minority—almost 12 percent is African American and almost 38 percent is Latino.[6] Arizona, where almost 30 percent of the state is Latino, is another state that, like Nevada, could become a battleground state because of an increase in the Latino population. In the nine states where the Latino population increased by 100 percent or more between 2000 and 2010, seven went Republican in the 2008 presidential election.[7] These demographic changes could have

TABLE 7-1. Demographics of Battleground States, 2010,
and Change since 2000
Percent

State	African Americans		Latinos		Asians	
	Share 2010	Change since 2000	Share 2010	Change since 2000	Share 2010	Change since 2000
CO	4	22	21	41	3	46
FL	16	28	23	57	2	71
IN	9	16	6	82	2	73
IA	3	44	5	84	2	45
MO	12	10	4	79	2	59
MT	0.4	50	3	58	0.6	33
NV	8	61	27	82	7	117
NH	1	66	3	79	2	78
NM	2	24	46	25	1	50
NC	22	18	8	111	2	84
OH	12	8	3	63	2	45
PA	11	13	6	83	3	59
TX	12	24	38	42	4	72
VA	19	12	8	92	6	69
WI	6	18	6	74	2	46

Source: U.S. Census Bureau (http://2010.census.gov/2010 census/data).

ramifications for decades to come. Almost one quarter—23 percent—of children age seventeen or younger are Latino. As these young people enter the electorate, they will expand the Democratic Party's base of support, unless the Republican Party can do a better job than they have in the past in appealing to Latinos.

AN INCREASINGLY DIVERSE ELECTORATE

Table 7-2 looks at turnout in presidential elections between 1968 and 2008 for African Americans, Latinos, young people ages eighteen to twenty-four, and women and turnout from 1996 on among Asians.[8] As the table shows, there was no noticeable trend in turnout among any of these groups between 1968 and 1996. Turnout among African

TABLE 7-2. Voting in Presidential Elections, 1968–2008
Percent

Year	African American	Latino	Asian	Ages 18–24	Women	White
1968[a]	58	n.a.	n.a.	50[b]	66	69
1972	52	38	n.a.	50	62	65
1976	49	32	n.a.	42	59	61
1980	51	30	n.a.	40	59	61
1984	56	33	n.a.	41	61	61
1988	52	29	n.a.	36	58	59
1992	54	29	n.a.	43	62	64
1996	51	27	45	32	56	56
2000[c]	57	45	43	36	61	60
2004[d]	60	47	44	47	65	65
2008[e]	65	50	48	49	66	64

a. Data for 1968–96: U.S. Census Bureau, Current Population Reports, P20-504, July 1998.
b. Indicates 21–24-year-olds, except 18–24 in Georgia and Kentucky, 19–24 in Alaska, and 20–24 in Hawaii.
c. U.S. Census Bureau, Current Population Reports, P20-542, February 2002.
d. U.S. Census Bureau, Current Population Reports, P20-556, March 2006.
e. U.S. Census Bureau, Current Population Reports, P20-563, May 2010.
n.a. = Not available.

Americans went from a high of 57.6 percent in 1968 to a low of 48.7 percent eight years later and then hovered between 50 and 55 percent between 1980 and 1996. Between a quarter and a third of Latinos voted in the presidential elections between 1968 and 1996.[9] Turnout among the youngest segment of the electorate historically has been the lowest of any age group. Turnout among this demographic group was at its highest in the period between 1972 and 1996 in 1972, shortly after the ratification of the Twenty-Sixth Amendment. Just under 50 percent (49.6 percent) of eighteen-to-twenty-four-year-olds voted in the 1972 presidential election; this dropped in 1996 to slightly less than a third of all of this age group.

The one demographic group that did change in this period was women. Historically, men turn out at higher rates than women, but in 1984 the turnout of women exceeded that of men: 61 percent of women voted, compared to 59 percent of men. Since 1984 women have turned out to vote in presidential elections in greater numbers than men.

Beginning with the 2000 election, turnout among African Americans, Latinos, and eighteen-to-twenty-four-year-olds began to increase. African American turnout increased from just over 50 percent in 1996 to 56.8 percent in 2000, to 60 percent in 2004, and then to a record 64.7 percent in 2008. Turnout among Latinos jumped from 26.7 in 1996 to 45.1 percent in 2000, with more modest increases in 2004 (47.2 percent) and 2008 (49.9 percent). Just under one-third of eighteen-to-twenty-four-year-olds turned out to vote in 1996, and over one-third voted in the 2000 election (36.1 percent). Turnout among this group jumped by ten percentage points from 2000 to 2004, and in the 2008 election almost half, 48.5 percent, of them voted. Turnout among Asians also increased between the 2000 and 2008 elections, from 43.3 percent to 47.6 percent.

The 2008 electorate was the most diverse in the history of the United States. The Pew Research Center finds that the number of African Americans and Latinos who reported voting in the 2008 election increased by 4 million over those who reported voting in the 2004 election (2 million more African Americans and 2 million more Latinos). Among African American women, turnout increased from 63.7 percent to 68.8 percent. The study also finds that 338,000 more Asians voted in 2008 than in 2004. In 2008 one-quarter of the electorate was nonwhite, the largest percentage in American history, and 2 million more people under age thirty voted in 2008 than in 2004. Among African Americans between eighteen and twenty-nine, turnout was 58 percent, an increase of almost 20 percent from the 2000 presidential election.[10]

Expanding the Electorate

While a more diverse U.S. population may lead to a more diverse electorate, the Obama campaign recognized that it had to work to mobilize demographic groups that traditionally did not turn out in high numbers, specifically African Americans, young people, and Latinos. There had been a significant increase in turnout by eighteen-to-twenty-nine-year-olds in the 2004 election, a 9.3 increase from 2000, or about 52 percent of the overall youth population.[11] The campaign thought that the possibility of the first African American president would draw African Americans to participate in the election. The campaign also saw Latinos as a demographic group that could be energized, particularly in western states such as Nevada, Colorado, and New Mexico. The campaign thought that changes in election laws and new means to communicate with voters through social media could be used to expand the electorate.

One of the first strategic decisions the Obama campaign made was that, to win the nomination, it had to first change the electorate, particularly among Iowa caucus-goers. As David Plouffe describes the campaign's thinking:

> From the get-go it was clear we could not win if the caucus universe was the same as it was in 2004. . . . To win, we would have to attain . . . a fundamentally altered electorate. . . . We had to grow the share of the electorate we believed would be most supportive of Obama. The 2008 caucuses would have to be younger, attended by more minorities.[12]

The Iowa caucuses in past elections had had higher attendance among older adults than among other demographic groups. As Plouffe observes, "In every recent caucus, twice as many people over sixty-five had turned out as people under thirty." Plouffe decided early on in the campaign that, rather than campaigning among traditional Iowa caucus-goers—Democratic Party activists, those who attended party fundraisers and other organized activities—Obama would reach out to nontraditional groups, Independents, and even Republicans.[13] At first, even the Obama campaign staff in Iowa was skeptical of this strategy. Mitch Stewart, the Obama campaign's Iowa caucus director, describes the reaction of the staff as follows: "We were a bit skeptical ourselves of this plan to bring in all these new caucus-goers . . . just based on the lore of Iowa—you know, that there's a certain set of groups that generally shows up and it's our responsibility to persuade those folks as opposed to bringing in a whole new slew of people." Plouffe and Paul Tewes, the Obama campaign's Iowa state director, wanted to reach out to not only Independents and Republicans but also unregistered Iowans, "African Americans, veterans, farmers, labor, Latinos, teachers, women, gays and lesbians, environmentalists, sportsmen, Native Americans, the disabled, peace groups—and most importantly, young voters."

One reason Plouffe and Tewes felt confident in their strategy to expand the Iowa caucus-going electorate was because many of Obama's top campaign staff had experience in Iowa in prior elections. Plouffe had been a staffer to former House majority leader Richard Gephardt, who had run for president in both 1988 and 2004 and thus had experience with the Iowa caucus process. Tewes was Al Gore's field director in Iowa during the 2000 election. Stewart had been a regional field director for the Edwards campaign in 2004. David Axelrod, the campaign's top strategist, had worked on Iowa governor Tom Vilsack's campaigns and on the presidential campaigns of Senators Paul Simon in 1988 and John Edwards in 2004. At least half a dozen other key Iowa staffers had experience in Iowa before 2008.[14]

For the Obama campaign, caucus success would come only if it got people to attend the caucus who had never caucused before or had never before been registered to vote, particularly young people. Because the caucuses were occurring so early, many college students were still at home for Christmas vacation. Dan Balz and Haynes Johnson describe how the Obama campaign kept track of these student supporters: "During the Christmas holidays [the Obama campaign] had devised elaborate means of tracking college-age students, handing them off from an organizer at their campus town to an organizer in their hometown."[15]

In the end, the Obama campaign's strategy of expanding the Iowa caucus-going electorate paid off. Turnout exceeded both the Obama and Clinton campaigns' expectations. The Clinton campaign had estimated turnout at about 150,000; the Obama campaign estimated it at between 167,000 and 180,000.[16] In fact, 239,872 Iowans turned out to caucus on January 3. David Plouffe describes the scene at one caucus site: "There was an elderly man with a long white beard and a red T-shirt who looked like Gandalf from *The Lord of the Rings*. There were young African Americans and single moms and families." When former Iowa governor Tom Vilsack, a Clinton supporter, walked into his caucus, his first reaction was "Who are these people? . . . I've never seen these people before."

The strategy of expanding the electorate worked in states beyond Iowa. The campaign registered thousands of new voters in both Indiana and North Carolina, traditionally Republican states, and most of the new registrants were African Americans and younger voters.[17] Not only did the campaign increase registration among these groups, but these voters also turned out in the primaries in numbers that flouted the conventional wisdom that new registrants are less likely to vote than those who have participated in past elections.

The strategic decision to expand the electorate continued into the general election, particularly in the battleground states. David Plouffe describes the campaign's thinking about the electorate in the general election:

> If we did not register enough African Americans and young voters in North Carolina and then turn them out on Election Day, we could not win. Facing a traditional electorate meant we shouldn't even bother with a state like North Carolina, no matter how much money we spent. . . . Colorado and Nevada were great takeaway opportunities. Neither state broke Democratic or was particularly close in 2000 or 2004, but the growing influence of Latino voters and Obama's appeal with western independents gave us a great shot to pick them both up. Expanding the electorate through voter registration could have a meaningful effect in both states, and we thought younger voters could really help juice turnout favorably.[18]

Virginia is a historically Republican state but one that elected Democratic governors in 2001 and 2005 and Democratic senators in 2006 and 2008. David Plouffe describes it as a key to the Obama strategy in 2008. "Virginia was a cornerstone to our strategy. . . . Wresting Virginia from McCain would severely limit his options. He would have to win a large Kerry state or the race was over."[19] Virginia was the first state Obama visited after he won the nomination, and it was where he had his last campaign rally on election eve. As seen above, Virginia is a good example of the changing demographics in the United States. The African American population in Virginia increased 11.6 percent between 2000 and 2010, and African Americans now make up almost 20 percent of the state's population. The Asian population increased 68.5 percent (5.5 percent of Virginians identified themselves as Asian in 2010), and the Latino population almost doubled (almost 8 percent of the state's population is Latino).[20]

MOBILIZING THE ELECTORATE

Just as the Obama campaign's strategy in 2008 was to change the electorate, the Bush campaign in 2004 also decided it needed to change the electorate from those who had voted in 2000. Karl Rove, the architect of Bush's 2000 and 2004 campaigns, felt that if more evangelical Christians had turned out to vote in 2000, Bush could have won the nationwide popular vote. The Bush campaign used microtargeting, a process that uses commercial data to divide the population into segments based on their consumer habits, to find Republicans in precincts that were primarily Democratic, and then to develop a turnout operation to get these likely Republican voters to the polls. Matthew Dowd, the pollster for the Bush campaign, describes how this combination of microtargeting and turnout worked:

> Republican firms . . . delved into commercial databases that pinpointed consumer buying patterns and television-watching habits to unearth such information as Coors beer and bourbon drinkers skewing Republican, brandy and cognac drinkers tilting Democratic; college football TV viewers were more Republican than those who watched professional football; viewers of Fox News were overwhelmingly committed to vote for Bush; homes with telephone caller ID tended to be Republican; people interested in gambling, fashion, and theater tended to be Democratic.
>
> Surveys of people on these consumer data lists were then used to determine "anger points" (late-term abortion, trial lawyer fees, estate taxes) that coincided with the Bush agenda for as many as 32 categories of voters, each identifiable by income, magazine subscriptions, favorite television shows and other "flags." Merging this data, in turn, enabled those running direct mail, precinct walking and phone bank programs to target each voter with a tailored message.[21]

Historically, Democrats had always done a more effective job of turning out their supporters on Election Day—so-called get-out-the-vote operations. Such operations were more important for Democrats because the Democratic base consisted of demographic groups less likely to vote, such as African Americans, those with lower incomes, and urban residents. However, following the 2000 presidential election, Karl Rove wanted to see if there was a way to increase the turnout of Republicans. In the off-year election in New Jersey in 2001, the Republican Party tested various get-out-the-vote efforts and found that door-to-door canvassing was the most effective in increasing turnout. Research by the political scientists Donald Green and Alan Gerber shows the same thing: "The more personal the interaction between campaign and potential voter, the more it raises a person's chance of voting."[22] Moreover, "door-to-door canvassing by friends and neighbors is the gold-standard mobilization tactic."

Using the findings of their research in New Jersey in 2001, the Republican Party developed the 72 Hour Project, a get-out-the-vote effort, and used it successfully in several congressional and Senate races in 2002. In 2004 the Republican Party and the Bush campaign continued the 72 Hour Project but made the strategic decision to train Republicans in their neighborhoods as team leaders, who would then organize their friends and neighbors to support President Bush. In contrast, in 2004 the Democratic Party and the Kerry campaign relied on organizations such as organized labor and America Coming Together to carry out their get-out-the-vote operation. Howard Dean describes the consequences of the different strategies to the outcome of the election in Ohio in 2004: "We ran the best grassroots campaign that I've seen in my lifetime. They ran a better one. Why? Because we sent 14,000 people into Ohio from elsewhere. They had 14,000 people from Ohio talking to their neighbors, and that's how you can win."[23]

The Democrats learned their lesson in 2004. When he became chair of the Democratic National Committee following the 2004 election, Dean created a fifty-state strategy aimed at developing local leaders in each of the states. The Obama campaign's grassroots strategy also used this more local focus. David Plouffe describes the importance of this strategy in Indiana, a historically Republican state that Obama carried in 2008: "We could not convert enough Indiana Republicans unless we had their neighbors talking to them about why they were supporting Obama, explaining his positions and defending him against McCain's attacks."[24]

The Obama campaign also took advantage of the opportunities for early voting in many states in 2008 to mobilize its electorate. Balz and Johnson describe how this worked:

Their goal was to bank as many votes as possible before election day—especially voters who were newly registered or had participated only sporadically in the past. Anyone following state-by-state statistics could see the strategy was working. In Colorado, more than half the total votes were cast before election day. . . . In Florida, more than a third of the total 2004 votes were cast early. . . .

In Nevada, more than half of the 2004 vote was cast early. . . . In North Carolina, Democrats had a big margin among early voters as the Republican turnout dropped dramatically.[25]

The Obama campaign's investment in new media gave it opportunities to reach out to new voters, particularly young people. The Obama campaign used every opportunity to collect e-mail addresses, cell phone numbers, and social networking links. By the end of the campaign 13 million people were on the campaign's e-mail list; it had 3 million Facebook friends, 2 million MySpace friends, and more than 100,000 people following the campaign on Twitter.[26] This enormous grassroots effort enabled the campaign to reach and mobilize potential supporters.

CONCLUSION

Between 1968 and 2008 the demographics of the United States changed. The percentage of the country made up of minorities, particularly African Americans and Latinos, grew. Between 2000 and 2008 the participation of these two groups in presidential elections, as well as that of young people ages eighteen to twenty-nine, also grew. The 2008 electorate was the most diverse in the country's history, both because of the changing demographics in the country and because of the Obama campaign's efforts to involve African Americans, Latinos, and young people in the election in numbers unprecedented in previous elections.

CHAPTER EIGHT

LOOKING TOWARD 2012

IN THE LATE WINTER/EARLY spring of 2007 the electoral playing field for the 2008 election had begun to take shape. By then both Barack Obama and Hillary Clinton had announced their candidacies for the Democratic nomination, as had John Edwards. On the Republican side, the field also had largely taken shape, though John McCain didn't formally announce his candidacy until April.

Four years later—by mid-February of 2011—the Republican field remained wide open, though at least a dozen candidates were being prominently mentioned as possible candidates. Some of these, however, did announce their intention not to run, among them Indiana representative Mike Pence, South Dakota senator John Thune, former Florida governor Jeb Bush, and New Jersey governor Chris Christie. Only one potential candidate for the Republican nomination—Herman Cain—had declared his candidacy, and he was not expected to be a top-tier candidate when the race began. In March the former Minnesota governor Tim Pawlenty became the first major Republican candidate when he announced the creation of an exploratory committee. And in a sign of the role that social media will play in the 2012 election, Pawlenty made his announcement in a video posted on Facebook.[1]

Meanwhile, President Obama had begun to plan his reelection; his headquarters would once again, as in 2008, be in Chicago. Key staff had begun to move back to Chicago—David Axelrod, as a key strategist; Jim Messina, former deputy chief of staff at the White House, as campaign manager; Juliana Smoot, national fundraising chair for the Obama campaign in 2008 and White House social secretary in 2009, as a deputy campaign manager with a focus on fundraising; and Jennifer O'Malley Dillon, former executive director of the Democratic National Committee and a voter-targeting expert, also as a deputy campaign manager.[2]

Obama was the first candidate in the 2012 election to formally announce as a candidate, which he did on April 4, 2011. It was another two months before the Republican field came into focus. In fact, there were so few Republican candidates in the race by spring that the Ronald Reagan Presidential Foundation moved a debate it was cosponsoring with NBC and Politico from May 2 to September 7. In postponing the debate the executive director of the Reagan Foundation said, "Although there will be a long and impressive list of Republican candidates who eventually take the field, too few have made the commitment thus far for a debate to be worthwhile in early May."[3]

The first Republican debate looking to the 2012 election was held on May 5, 2011, in South Carolina, one of the early primary states. Only Pawlenty, the former Pennsylvania senator Rick Santorum, Representative Ron Paul, Herman Cain, and the former New Mexico governor Gary Johnson took part. Aside from Pawlenty, no first-tier candidate participated.[4] In contrast, the first Republican debate four years earlier had included ten contenders for the nomination, including Mitt Romney, Mike Huckabee, and John McCain.[5]

The Republican primary field finally began to take shape between mid-May and late June. The former House Speaker Newt Gingrich entered the race on May 11, followed by Ron Paul on May 13. Tim Pawlenty formally announced his candidacy on May 23, Mitt Romney on June 2, and Rick Santorum on June 6. The former Utah governor Jon Huntsman jumped into the race on June 21, just weeks after stepping down as the Obama administration's U.S. Ambassador to China. Representative Michelle Bachmann announced her candidacy on June 27.[6]

One test of the relative strength of the Republican contenders is each candidate's fundraising total for the first two quarters of 2011, particularly the second quarter, when the field was more established. Not surprisingly, Mitt Romney led the field in the second quarter, raising $18.25 million between April 1 and June 30, over four times more than any other Republican candidate.[7] During the same time period Ron Paul raised

$4.5 million, Tim Pawlenty $4.2 million, and Jon Huntsman $4.1 million.[8] Huntsman's $4.1 million included a personal donation to his campaign; the exact amount Huntsman donated was not reported—his campaign would only say that the donation was "less than half" of the total amount raised.[9] Michelle Bachmann raised $3.6 million during the second quarter.[10] Newt Gingrich and Herman Cain raised even less than Paul, Pawlenty, and Huntsman—$2 million and $2.5 million, respectively.[11]

Barack Obama's fundraising in the second quarter dwarfed the fundraising of his potential Republican opponents. Obama raised $47 million for his reelection campaign, and another $38 million for the Democratic National Committee.[12] Obama's $47 million both set a record for fundraising during the second quarter of the year before a presidential election and exceeded the combined amount raised by the Republicans seeking the nomination at the time.

The second test of the strength of the Republican field in the summer before the election year is the Iowa straw poll, held in mid-August. The Iowa straw poll is not really a poll at all but rather a fundraiser for the Iowa Republican Party. Nevertheless, it is seen as a measure of the organizational strengths of the Republican candidates, as they try to get as many of their supporters as possible to attend and vote. Romney, Huntsman, and Gingrich chose not to compete in the 2012 Iowa straw poll, so the poll shaped up as a contest between Tim Pawlenty, who had been campaigning for the nomination for two years, and Michelle Bachman, a relative newcomer to the race. Bachman won the straw poll with 29 percent of the vote; Pawlenty finished a distant third, with 14 percent of the vote (Ron Paul finished second with 28 percent of the vote). A day after the straw poll Pawlenty dropped out of the race for the Republican nomination.

The Republican field shifted again in mid-August. Not only was Pawlenty out of the race, but Texas governor Rick Perry announced that he would be a candidate for the nomination. Perry quickly moved to the front of the pack in the run for the nomination; a Gallup poll in late August showed him with 29 percent of the vote, compared to Romney's 17 percent, among Republicans and Republican-leaning independents.[13] Perry was also expected to rival Romney in his fundraising abilities; he raised more than $39 million for his 2010 reelection.[14]

THE NOMINATION PROCESS

At their respective conventions in 2008 both the Democratic and Republican Parties created commissions to look into the delegate selection process for the 2012 elections. The Republican Party's commission, the Temporary Delegate Selection Committee, was charged with looking at the timing of the nomination process; the Democratic Party's commission, the Democratic Change Commission, was charged with examining the role of superdelegates and considering ways to improve the caucus process. It was also to look at the timing of the nomination process. In an unprecedented move in nomination reform efforts, the two commissions agreed to come up with a 2012 timetable that both parties would use.[15]

As a result, both parties agreed to a 2012 primary and caucus schedule that pushes primaries and caucuses later in the spring. Iowa, New Hampshire, South Carolina, and Nevada could schedule their respective primaries and caucuses on or after February 1, 2012; all other states could not schedule their primaries and caucuses until, at the earliest, the first Tuesday in March.[16] However, it is one thing for Democratic and Republican Parties to mandate the window for the primaries and caucuses, it is another thing to get the states to agree. As chapter 2 illustrates, several states in 2008 moved their primaries and caucuses outside the window established by the parties. By the spring of 2011 there were already signs that similar activity could occur in 2012. In 2008 the Florida primary was held in January; Republican state legislators initially pushed to have the primary held in January again in 2012, even though Democratic and Republican Party rules require that the primary be held after March 6.[17] Were Florida to schedule its primary before March 6, it would lose half its delegates to the Republican National Convention. By summer there was talk of moving the primary to March 1, 2, or 3, which would put the Florida primary after those of Iowa, New Hampshire, South Carolina, and Nevada but still outside the March 6 window mandated by the political parties.[18]

The Republican Party also required that in states that schedule primaries and caucuses before April 1 all delegates must be selected on a proportional basis, a change from the winner-take-all option afforded states in past elections.[19] The proportional representation provision could have a substantial impact on the Republican nomination. First, it will make it more difficult for any one candidate to wrap up the nomination early. Chapter 2 describes how McCain was able to take advantage of the winner-take-all system in 2008 to become the presumptive Republican nominee on February 5. With a crowded Republican field in 2012, proportional representation in the early months will likely extend the nomination process farther into the spring. Second, a proportional representation system may encourage states to schedule their primaries and caucuses later in the spring, when states can implement winner-take-all systems, which could give the states more influence in the nomination process, because candidates can amass delegates more quickly.

The Democratic National Committee also put in provisions encouraging states to schedule primaries and caucuses later in the spring. Bonus delegates will be awarded to states that schedule primaries later or that work to create regional primaries and caucuses. The DNC created three time periods for states to choose from, each with its own rewards: March 6–31, April 1–30, and May 1–June 12. As states move their primaries into the later slots, they can increase their number of delegates to the convention. The increase is 10 percent in the earliest category and 20 percent in the latest category. States that cluster their primaries and caucuses into regions will receive 15 percent more delegates above their base allocation.[20]

The Democratic Change Commission also addressed the role of superdelegates. Between 1984, when superdelegates were created, and 2008, the commission argued, there had been an "enhanced level of public participation in . . . primaries and caucuses," such that there was no longer a need for superdelegates.[21] The commission recommends that a new category of delegates be created. These delegates would be those people who previously had been superdelegates (DNC members, members of the House and Senate, governors, and other party leaders) but would be pledged (rather than unpledged) delegates. These new delegates would be called National Pledged Party Leader and Elected Official (NPLEO) delegates and would be allocated to presidential candidates based on the primary or caucus results in each state. Anyone in this category who did not want to be a pledged delegate could still attend the convention— but as a nonvoting delegate. In essence, this change would have eliminated the possibility that superdelegates could change the outcome of the nomination process, as the Clinton campaign tried to do in its courting of superdelegates in 2008. However, in the end the DNC rejected the recommendations of the Change Commission. It voted to retain the role of superdelegates as unpledged delegates but to reduce the percentage of superdelegates at the convention by 5 percent (from 20 percent to 15 percent of the delegates).[22]

Finally, the Democratic Change Commission addressed the issue of caucuses. The Change Commission report summarizes the several concerns about caucus participation as follows: "There is a participation barrier in caucuses which limits the ability of the elderly, shift workers, students, members of the military and others with certain hindrances on their ability to take part in the process. For those who are unable to attend the meeting during which the caucus is held, there is currently no way to cast a ballot."[23] The Change Commission recommends that a set of best practices be created for caucus states to use. The Rules and Bylaws Committee of the DNC was charged with overseeing the development of these best practices and with monitoring states to ensure that best practices were being met.

The Conventions

Both parties have chosen to have their 2012 conventions in states that played pivotal roles in past elections. The Republican Party's convention will be in Tampa, Florida, the state that decided the election in 2000 and that was a battleground state in both 2004 and 2008. The Democratic Party's convention will be in Charlotte, North Carolina, the one play-hard state that the Clinton campaign lost in 1992. It is also a state that the Democratic Party carried in 2008 for the first time since 1976, in large part because of African American voters, whose turnout in North Carolina increased just over 6 percent from 2004 to 2008.[24] The DNC also announced that it will not accept corporate or PAC contributions to fund the convention, nor will it accept any contributions over $100,000. By stating that the convention would be funded by "grassroots activists and rank-and-file party members," the themes of the 2012 Obama campaign, and the contrast with whoever is the Republican Party nominee, began to emerge.[25] The Obama campaign seems to be trying to recapture the insurgent, from-the-people, spirit of the 2008 campaign.

The Electoral College

The reapportionment of House seats following the 2010 census, and the consequent shifting of Electoral College votes in each state, will change the Electoral College map in 2012. Of the ten states losing Electoral College votes, eight were carried by Obama in 2008, and collectively those states will lose ten Electoral College votes. Of the eight states gaining Electoral College votes, five were carried by McCain in 2008, and those states will gain eight Electoral College votes. Nevada, Florida, and Washington, states carried by Obama in 2008, will pick up a total of four Electoral College votes. The two states losing Electoral College votes that went for McCain in 2008, Louisiana and Missouri, will only lose, between them, two Electoral College votes. In sum, that is a net loss of six Obama Electoral College votes and a net gain of six Electoral College votes for the Republican candidate, for a swing of twelve Electoral College votes in favor of the Republican candidate in 2012.

Given Obama's large Electoral College vote in 2008, a loss of twelve would still give him a healthy Electoral College victory in 2012. However, the changes in the Electoral College votes in each state will likely change the calculus of both party nominees in terms of their determination of battleground states. What will also affect the Electoral College map in 2012 is the changing nature of the electorate. As shown in chapter 7, many of the states with increasing Electoral College votes also have increases in minority populations, which tend to vote Democratic.

Role of Technology

Technological innovations will likely play an important role in the 2012 elections, as they did in those of 2008. A study by the Pew Research Center finds that of the 60 percent of American adults who used social networking sites such as Facebook and MySpace in 2010, 35 percent used those sites to get information about politics or political campaigns.[26] Young people ages eighteen to twenty-nine were most likely to use social networking sites for political purposes; 42 percent reported doing so, suggesting that these sites will again play an important role in engaging the youngest demographic cohort. The study finds no differences in the percentages of Democrats and Republicans who used social networking sites for political purposes, which is a change from 2008, when Obama supporters were more likely to use social networking sites for political purposes than were McCain supporters. Twitter was also used to engage in political activity in 2010 but to a lesser degree than social networking sites: 28 percent of Twitter users reported using Twitter to engage in the 2010 elections in some fashion.

When asked why they use these sites to follow candidates or other political groups, the most common response is that they make the respondents "feel more personally connected to the candidates or groups they follow."[27] As tools for reaching groups who historically have felt disconnected from politics, these sites will likely play an important role in engaging these groups in the 2012 elections. Some candidates announced the creation of exploratory committees and their candidacies on Twitter and Facebook, and the first Twitter debate occurred among some of the Republican candidates in July 2011.

THE CANDIDATES

In 2009 a new political movement, the Tea Party (for Taxed Enough Already) sprang up, and Tea Party candidates offered challenges—some successful, some not—to Republican congressional candidates in the 2010 midterm elections. The large Republican presidential field reflects the influence of the Tea Party, with some candidates aligned with that party, such as Michelle Bachmann, who created and chairs the House of Representatives Tea Party Caucus, and other candidates, such as Mitt Romney, aligned with more traditional forces in the Republican Party.

One of the questions going into the nomination process is how these two factions within the Republican Party will fare during the nomination process. A *Washington Post*–ABC News poll in mid-2011 shows Mitt Romney leading among all Republicans and GOP-leaning independents, with 26 percent saying that they would support him in the primary or caucus in their state. However, among strong Tea Party supporters, 23 percent favor Michelle Bachmann, compared to just 12 percent of all Republican and GOP-leaning independents who support Bachmann. Among strong Tea Party supporters, just 18 percent favor Romney.[28]

When the Republicans picked up sixty-three House seats in the 2010 midterm elections—and with that, control of the House of Representatives—and in addition picked up six seats in the Senate, Obama's prospects for reelection in 2012 looked questionable. In a postelection press conference Obama himself described his party's losses as a "shellacking." For much of 2010 his job performance ratings hovered just below 50 percent, and he didn't seem to be getting credit with the American people for his signature accomplishments—health care reform and reform of the financial industry. Yet a remarkably bipartisan and productive lame duck session of Congress following the 2010 elections—along with a moving speech in Tucson, Arizona, following the shootings that killed six people and wounded thirteen others, including Arizona congresswoman Gabrielle Giffords—seemed to shore up Obama's job approval ratings.

Two and a half years into his presidency Obama's job approval rating was 47 percent, less than George W. Bush's approval rating at the same time in his presidency (64 percent) but only slightly less than Bill Clinton's (49 percent) and above Ronald Reagan's (44 percent).[29] All of them were reelected to a second term. A key to Obama's reelection prospects will certainly be the performance of the economy. An improved economic picture, particularly in terms of jobs, will help Obama's reelection chances. His prospects in 2012 will also depend on his ability to reignite the excitement among newcomers to the electorate in 2008, particularly young people and African Americans, and to capitalize on the growing Latino population.

OUTSIDE GROUPS

One thing that will distinguish the 2012 presidential election from the 2008 election is the role of outside groups in the election. While outside groups played some role in the 2004 election, as seen in chapter 4, outside groups will likely play an even larger role in the 2012 election. A U.S. Supreme Court decision in January 2010, *Citizens United* v. *Federal Election Commission* (commonly referred to as the *Citizens United* decision), rules that corporations (and implicitly unions and nonprofit groups) have the same free speech rights as individuals, meaning that they can spend unlimited amounts of money in political campaigns. According to the Campaign Finance Institute, nonparty groups spent $280 million on independent expenditures and electioneering communications in 2010, a 130 percent increase over spending by such groups in 2008.[30]

Spending by these outside groups occurred in primarily two forms: spending by newly created super PACs, which can accept unlimited funds from any donor as long as the donors are disclosed to the Federal Election Commission and the super PAC does not coordinate its spending with candidates; and spending by nonprofit groups, which are not required to disclose their donors. The most prolific spending in 2010 among such outside groups was by American Crossroads, a super PAC founded by, among others, Karl Rove, a key adviser to President George W. Bush, and Crossroads GPS, a nonprofit group. American Crossroads raised almost $28 million in 2010, and Crossroads GPS raised another $43 million.[31]

Eighteen months before the 2012 general election American Crossroads and Crossroads GPS indicated that they intended to be major players in both the presidential and congressional elections of 2012, pledging to spend at least $120 million during the election cycle.[32] In late June 2011, Crossroads GPS began spending $5 million on television and radio ads in ten states, ostensibly to influence the debate taking place at the time over raising the debt ceiling but clearly also aimed at influencing public perceptions of President Obama going into the 2012 election.

The Obama campaign discouraged spending by outside groups on behalf of the campaign in 2008, as mentioned in chapter 1. But it also decided that, to counter the conservative super PACs that formed in 2010 following the *Citizens United* decision, the campaign would not discourage the creation of super PACs on the Democratic side. Three super PACs were formed in the spring of 2011 to help elect Democratic candidates, including President Obama. Majority PAC would focus on electing Democratic Senate candidates, House Majority PAC would play the same role for Democratic House candidates, and Priorities USA Action would focus on the presidential race. A fourth group, American Bridge 21st Century, would focus on opposition research.[33] Majority PAC and American Bridge 21st Century plan to have a nonprofit component, similar to the American Crossroads and Crossroads GPS model.[34] Priorities USA Action began running ads in South Carolina in May, targeting Mitt Romney.[35] In late June it began running ads to counter those run by Crossroads GPS, though the Priorities' ad buy was less than that of Crossroads GPS—only $750,000—and ran in only five of the ten states targeted by Crossroads.[36]

In another sign of just how important money from outside groups could be in the 2012 election, a super PAC, Restore Our Future, was formed by supporters of Mitt Romney. Federal law limits contributions to Romney's campaign to $2,500 in the primary and, should he get the nomination, in the general election, but there will be no limits on contributions from Restore Our Future PAC. The downside for the Romney campaign, and the major reason Obama discouraged outside groups on his behalf in 2008, is that a super PAC cannot coordinate with the campaign.

CONCLUSION

President Obama heads into the 2012 election with a clear fundraising advantage over his opponents, an extensive list of past supporters, a seasoned campaign team, and expertise in putting together a successful campaign organization. Yet the political environment—the stubborn economy, intense partisanship, and an uncertainty that he can recapture the enthusiasm of the 2008 campaign—raise questions about his reelection. For the Republicans, the battle between the Tea Party and the more traditional party supporters will likely play out in the nomination process, which may well be more protracted due to changes in the process. Whoever gets the nomination will have to figure out how to appeal to all factions within the party. One thing is certain, whatever the political situation looks like eighteen months before the election is not a predictor of what might happen on Election Day, as the elections of 1980 and 1992 illustrate so well.

CHAPTER NINE

CONCLUSION

BETWEEN 1968 AND 2008 presidential elections in the United States became more democratic. More Americans had the opportunity to participate in the political process, and their participation became more open and transparent. Reforms occurred in the way elections are financed, conducted, and administered, and the electorate itself became more diverse. This chapter examines the state of presidential elections on the eve of the 2012 election.

CAMPAIGN FINANCE

Perhaps the most stubborn area for the democratization of presidential elections is campaign finance. For every reform of the campaign finance system there have been developments that allow large, and in some cases undisclosed, contributions back into the election process. The Federal Elections Campaign Act of 1971, and its amendments in 1974, limited the role of wealthy individuals in federal campaigns and required the disclosure of contributions to federal campaigns. Between 1971 and 2008 the role of big money in presidential elections ebbed and flowed: in the 1980s a series of FEC advisory opinions allowed soft money into the system; the 2002 Bipartisan Campaign Finance Reform Act prohibited political parties from raising soft money, beginning with the 2004 presidential race;, and in 2003 the U.S. Supreme Court upheld those prohibitions in *McConnell* v. *Federal Election Commission*.

Not only did the reforms of the 1970s remove much of the large money from the presidential race, but they also provide public funding to support candidates. Public funding removes the dependence on private contributions and the private interests often connected with those contributions, for presidential candidates. Public funding also allows candidates without access to wealth—either their own or through their political connections—to successfully compete in presidential elections. Candidates who demonstrate support for their candidacies by attaining modest contributions from individuals have those contributions matched by the federal treasury, allowing their campaigns to move forward. While partial public funding, beginning in 2000, has played less and less a role in the nominating process and was almost nonexistent in 2008, the Internet made it easier for citizens to contribute to campaigns. Small contributions played an important role in funding the 2008 presidential election, particularly for the Obama campaign.

The 2012 election, however, may be much less democratic than those in the preceding forty years. The *Citizens United* decision allows outside groups to raise and spend unlimited amounts of money on elections, some of it undisclosed. As seen in the previous chapter, outside groups on both the progressive and the conservative sides of the ideological spectrum plan to play a significant role in the 2012 elections. Public funding, while still in place, will not be a factor in President Obama's reelection, and it is likely that his Republican opponent will eschew public funding as well, in hopes of keeping up with Obama's spending. Campaign finance reports through the first half of 2007 suggest the potential for lopsided fundraising between Obama and his opponent, making the role of outside groups to fill in that gap on the conservative side all the more important.

Going forward, if the role of outside groups continues to grow and candidates no longer rely on public funding either in the nomination period or in the general election, there could once again be a discrepancy between well-known candidates with an ability to raise large amounts of money and candidates with less access to funds. While the period between 1968 and 2008 saw few candidates spending their own money on elections, the ability to self-fund part of a campaign may be more important in 2012 and beyond. The opportunity to raise small contributions online could mitigate that, but candidates with access to wealth may once again dominate the presidential election process.

The Nomination Process

The nomination process also became more democratic between 1968 and 2008. Candidates were no longer chosen in closed-door caucuses and conventions but rather in large part in primaries open to all eligible voters. Even in states that still used caucuses, those caucuses were much more open and public.

Primaries and caucuses each have their strengths and weaknesses. Modern-day caucuses take place over several hours and require friends, neighbors, and co-workers to publicly declare their support for a candidate. Caucuses require strong organizational skills on the part of the campaign, to get supporters to the caucus and to keep them in attendance and supporting the campaign's candidate throughout the caucus. Candidates who have or can develop strong followings are often able to be successful in caucuses, even if they are not initially well known or do not have strong financial resources.

However, because caucuses occur at a set period in time, some individuals who would like to attend are precluded from doing so because of their personal situations—work, family, or health issues, for example. Some argue that caucuses are more democratic because they require people to debate the strengths and weaknesses of candidates in a public forum; others argue that caucuses are less democratic because some people, because of their personal situations, are precluded from attending. It is the latter argument that led the Democratic National Committee to charge the DNC's Rules and Bylaws Committee to develop a set of caucus best practices for the 2012 election.

Primaries allow for voting over an approximately twelve-hour period, making them better able to accommodate voters' personal situations and to also allow voting by absentee ballots for those unable to vote on primary day. Turnout is typically much higher in presidential primaries than at presidential caucuses, and primaries remain the most common method of choosing delegates to the national party conventions. Yet primaries can also favor better known and better funded candidates and can be more expensive for states to administer. Washington State "suspended" its 2012 presidential primary (the state hopes to resume the primary in 2016) to save the state over $10 million. The legislation to suspend the primary was bipartisan, supported by the Republican secretary of state, Sam Reed, and the Democratic governor, Chris Gregoire. Both expressed "their continuing support for the presidential primary as the preferred method for engaging the electorate in picking presidential favorites."[1]

THE CONVENTIONS AND THE GENERAL ELECTION

Between 1968 and 2008 the national nominating conventions became more scripted, with less news made at the conventions and the work of the party done more and more behind the scenes and out of view of both convention delegates and the general public. Network coverage of conventions plummeted, and cable coverage became more discussions by talking heads than coverage of the business of the convention. Yet the scripted nature of the conventions allowed the parties to present their candidates in their most favorable light and to kick off the start of the general election. Limited coverage meant limited time demands on the American public to watch the conventions—Americans could tune in to an hour of prime time coverage and see the two parties' nominees and their supporters. As chapter 3 points out, the 2008 Democratic and Republican conventions were the most watched conventions in the country's history.

The general elections between 1968 and 2008 saw a winnowing of states in which candidates waged their campaigns. More and more states fell into the "red" or "blue" category, leaving just a handful of battle-ground states, which prove to be a combination of large and small states throughout the country. The battleground states have changed during the forty-year period; Florida was not considered competitive in 1992, yet was the deciding state in the 2000 election. North Carolina, Virginia, and Colorado were not considered competitive in 2004 yet provided keys to the Obama victory in 2008.

While candidates concentrated their campaigns—both the air war and the ground war—in a handful of states, and the residents of those states saw the full-blown campaigns, the institutionalization of presidential and vice presidential debates by the Commission on Presidential Debates meant that all interested Americans would have opportunities to view the candidates several times during the general election. Moreover, over the forty-year period the debates changed from exchanges between candidates and journalists to opportunities for ordinary citizens to ask questions of the candidates. Social networking sites and social media expanded those opportunities in 2008, and the growth of both in the years to come will provide even more opportunities for citizens to question candidates in the debates.

POLITICAL PARTICIPATION AND A CHANGING ELECTORATE

The opportunities for Americans to participate in the presidential election process expanded dramatically between 1968 and 2008. Legislative and constitutional changes ended discriminatory practices and extended the right to vote to minorities and young people. Changes in election laws made it easier to vote through Election Day registration, convenience voting, and the use of provisional ballots. Both parties made strides to expand early primaries and caucuses beyond the largely white populated states of Iowa and New Hampshire to include South Carolina, with its large African American population, and Nevada, with its large Latino population. The political participation of African Americans, Latinos, Asians, young people, and women all increased, particularly in the latter part of the forty-year period.

The characteristics of candidates seeking the presidency also changed. No longer were presidential and vice presidential candidates white males. In 1984 Geraldine Ferraro became the first female major party vice presidential candidate. In 2008 the Democratic Party nominated an African American presidential candidate, and the Republican Party selected a female as its vice presidential nominee. An African American again heads the Democratic ticket in 2012, and the early Republican field includes both an African American and a woman.

Technological advancements over the forty-year period also increased opportunities for participation in presidential elections. Television became dominant, and the growth of cable television exponentially expanded opportunities both for citizens to receive information about candidates and campaigns and for candidates to communicate with potential voters. The rise of the Internet in the first decade of the twenty-first century again expanded opportunities for citizens to communicate with campaigns and for campaigns to reach out to potential supporters. Each election cycle brought new social networks and social media, and that will continue in the 2012 election and beyond.

However, going into the 2012 elections there are signs that some states are trying to constrict participation in elections. Legislation is making its way through state legislatures to require voter identification, to restrict voting by college students in states where they attend college but do not reside, to shorten early-voting windows, and to end Election Day registration. By the summer of 2011, Texas, Kansas, Wisconsin, and South Carolina had all enacted laws requiring voters to produce a state-issued voter identification card before they could vote, and Ohio and Pennsylvania were also considering voter ID laws.[2] Florida enacted legislation to reduce early voting from two weeks to one.[3] Maine, one of the first Election Day registration states, ended that practice, which had been in place for almost forty years.[4] Yet despite these efforts to potentially restrict voting, voting and registration laws are more democratic in 2012 than they were in 1968.

Finally, the American electorate has become more diverse over the past four decades. The 2010 census shows a growth in minorities, particularly Latinos. While minorities historically have not participated in elections to the degree that whites have, the 2000, 2004, and 2008 elections suggest increased participation in presidential elections. These elections also saw increased participation by young people.

CONCLUSION

The presidential election of 2012 will bear little resemblance to the 1968 election. Americans will have more opportunities to participate in the election, and the electorate will be more diverse. While the campaign finance system continues to challenge the democratization of presidential elections, the overall picture of presidential elections is one much more democratic than demonstrators faced in Grant Park in the summer of 1968.

Notes

Notes to Chapter 1

1. Herbert E. Alexander, *Financing Politics: Money, Elections, and Political Reform,* 4th ed. (Congressional Quarterly Press, 1992), pp. 24–29.

2. Since the inception of the Presidential Election Campaign Fund tax check-off system Americans have not been particularly enthusiastic about contributing to the fund. In 1976 just over one quarter (27.5 percent) checked the box on their tax return indicating a designation to the fund; by 2007, the last year that data are available from the FEC, the checkoff rate was under 10 percent. Federal Election Commission, "Presidential Fund Income Tax Check-Off Status, 1973–2010," January 2011. Legislation to provide federal subsidies to presidential candidates had passed the Congress in the 1960s but was never implemented. Herbert E. Alexander, *Financing Politics: Money, Elections, and Political Reform,* 2nd ed. (Congressional Quarterly Press, 1980), p. 28.

3. Alexander, *Financing Politics,* 2nd ed., p. 51.

4. The Tillman Act, enacted in 1907, banned corporate contributions to federal candidates. For illustrations of illegal corporate contributions to CREEP, see ibid., pp. 73–81.

5. The 1974 amendments also limited campaign expenditures, but those limits, except in the case of presidential campaigns that accepted public funds, were declared unconstitutional by the Supreme Court in *Buckley* v. *Valeo* in 1976.

6. Federal Election Commission, "FEC Approves Matching Funds for 2008 Presidential Candidates," news release, January 23, 2009.

7. See www.fec.gov/pages/brochures/pubfund_limits.2008.shtml.

8. Connolly spent $11 million and received one delegate to the Republican convention.

9. This figure excludes GELAC funds. With GELAC funds included, the primary spending limit in 2000 was $40.5 million.

10. Costas Panagopoulos and Daniel Bergan, "Contributions and Contributors in the 2004 Presidential Election," *Presidential Studies Quarterly* 36, no. 2 (2006): 155–71.

11. In 1996, however, Perot accepted $29.1 million in public funds in the general election, roughly half of what the major party candidates received that year. Anthony Corrado, "Public Funding of Presidential Campaigns," in *The New Campaign Finance Sourcebook,* edited by Anthony Corrado and others (Brookings, 2005), p. 194.

12. Kathleen Hall Jamieson, *Electing the President 2008: The Insider's View* (University of Pennsylvania Press, 2009), p. 66.

13. Herbert E. Alexander, *Financing the 1972 Election* (D.C. Heath, 1976), p. 88.

14. "Party Fundraising Escalates," Federal Election Commission, news release, January 12, 2001.

15. David B. Magleby, Anthony Corrado, and Kelly D. Patterson, eds., *Financing the 2004 Election* (Brookings, 2006), p. 11.

16. Ibid., p. 229.

17. Institute of Politics, John F. Kennedy School of Government, *Campaign for President: The Managers Look at 2004* (Rowman and Littlefield, 2006), pp. 215–16.

18. David B. Magleby, J. Quin Monson, and Kelly D. Patterson, *Dancing without Partners: How Candidates, Parties, and Interest Groups Interact in the New Campaign Finance Environment* (Center for the Study of Elections and Democracy, Brigham Young University, 2005), p. 35.

19. See www.nytimes.com/2007/04/02/us/politics/02campaign.html.

20. See www.npr.org/templates/story/story.php?storyId=9359779.

21. Sarah Cohen, Zachary A. Goldfarb, Seth Hamblin, and Laura Stanton, "A Closer Look at the Money," *Washington Post,* July 17, 2007, p. A6.

22. Sarah Cohen, Seth Hamblin, and Laura Stanton, "A Closer Look at the Money," *Washington Post,* October 17, 2007, p. A6; Sarah Cohen, "Money to Burn," *Washington Post,* February 2, 2008, p. A8.

23. Sarah Cohen, Zachary A. Goldfarb, Seth Hamblin, and Laura Stanton, "A Closer Look at the Money," *Washington Post,* April 17, 2007, p. A6.

24. Cohen, Hamblin, and Stanton, "A Closer Look at the Money"; Cohen, "Money to Burn."

25. Candice J. Nelson, "Strategies and Tactics of Fundraising in 2008," in *Campaigns and Elections American Style,* edited by James A. Thurber and Candice J. Nelson, 3rd ed. (Westview, 2009), pp. 94, 95.

26. Joshua Green, "The Front-Runner's Fall," *Atlantic Monthly,* September, 2008 (www.theatlantic.com/doc/print/200809/hillary-clinton-campaign).

27. Anthony Corrado, "Fundraising Strategies in the 2008 Presidential Campaign," in *Campaigns and Elections American Style,* edited by James A. Thurber and Candice J. Nelson, 3rd ed. (Westview, 2009), p. 114.

28. Ibid., p. 112.

29. See www.nytimes.com/2008/06/22/us/politics/22donate.html.

30. Corrado, "Fundraising Strategies in the 2008 Presidential Campaign," p. 125.

31. David B. Magleby and Anthony Corrado, eds., *Financing the 2008 Election* (Brookings, 2011), pp. 270, 271.

Notes to Chapter 2

1. Elaine C. Kamarck, *Primary Politics: How Presidential Candidates Have Shaped the Modern Nominating System* (Brookings, 2009), pp. 7–8.

2. Theodore H. White, *The Making of the President 1968* (Atheneum, 1969), p. 319.

3. Kamarck, *Primary Politics*, p. 14.

4. David E. Price, *Bringing Back the Parties* (Congressional Quarterly Press, 1984), p. 148.

5. Jeane Kirkpatrick, *The New Presidential Elite* (Russell Sage Foundation and Twentieth Century Fund, 1976), p. 328; for the percentages, see pp. 292–93.

6. Price, *Bringing Back the Parties*, p. 153.

7. William Crotty and John S. Jackson III, *Presidential Primaries and Nominations* (Congressional Quarterly Press, 1985), p. 33.

8. Patrick Healy, "Two Conventions with No Shortage of Contrasts," Political Memo, *New York Times Online,* September 3, 2008 (www.nytimes.com/2008/09/04/us/politics/04compare.html).

9. Price, *Bringing Back the Parties*, p. 148.

10. Crotty and Jackson, *Presidential Primaries and Nominations,* pp. 39, 40.

11. Kamarck, *Primary Politics*, p. 8.

12. White, *The Making of the President 1968*, p. 316.

13. Price, *Bringing Back the Parties*, p. 149.

14. Kamarck, *Primary Politics*, p. 13.

15. Crotty and Jackson, *Presidential Primaries and Nominations*, p. 34.

16. Price, *Bringing Back the Parties*, p. 152.

17. Ibid., p. 155.

18. Crotty and Jackson, *Presidential Primaries and Nominations*, pp. 34–35.

19. Kamarck, *Primary Politics*, p. 107.

20. Kirkpatrick, *The New Presidential Elite*, p. 47.

21. Kamarck, *Primary Politics*, p. 53.

22. Crotty and Jackson, *Presidential Primaries and Nominations*, pp. 46, 47.

23. See Kamarck, *Primary Politics*, pp. 82–83, for a description of these alternative methods.

24. For a description of the Republican rules, see ibid., pp. 82–84.

25. Gary C. Byrne and Paul Marx, *The Great American Convention: A Political History of Presidential Elections* (Pacific Books, 1976), pp. 121, 125–26, 128–33.

26. Jules Witcover, *Marathon: The Pursuit of the Presidency* (Viking Press, 1977), p. 214.

27. Kamarck, *Primary Politics,* p. 38.

28. William G. Mayer and Andrew E. Busch, *The Front-Loading Problem in Presidential Elections* (Brookings, 2004), p. 14.

29. Kamarck, *Primary Politics,* pp. 38–39. The following paragraphs also refer to this work; see ibid. pp. 72–73, 75.

30. Democratic National Committee, "Report of the Commission on Presidential Nomination Timing and Scheduling," 2004 (http://a9.g.akamai.net/7/9/8082/v001/democratic1.download.akamai.com/8082/pdfs/20051215_commission final.pdf).

31. Kamarck, *Primary Politics,* p. 77.

32. "A 'Very Personal Victory' for McCain in New Hampshire" (http://articles.cnn.com/2008-01-08/politics/nh.gop_1_independent-vote).

33. The Iowa Republican straw poll is not a poll at all but rather a test of organizational strength for candidates. Candidates recruit supporters, pay for their tickets to the event, and pay for their transportation to the event, which is basically a day-long picnic.

34. Michael D. Shear and Perry Bacon Jr., "Evangelicals Fuel Win over Romney," *Washington Post,* January 4, 2008, p. A1.

35. Michael D. Shear and Juliet Eilperin, "Romney 2nd in GOP Contest; Iowa Winner Huckabee Is 3rd," *Washington Post,* January 9, 2008, p. A1.

36. Dan Balz and Haynes Johnson, *The Battle for America 2008* (Penguin Group, 2009), p. 281.

37. Candice J. Nelson, "Campaigns Matter," in *Campaigns and Elections American Style,* edited by James A. Thurber and Candice J. Nelson, 3rd ed. (Westview, 2009), p. 306.

38. Balz and Johnson, *The Battle for America 2008,* p. 285.

39. William Kristol, *Fox News Sunday,* December 17, 2006, as reported in *Washington Post,* December 28, 2008, p. B2.

40. David Plouffe, *The Audacity to Win* (Penguin Group, 2009), p. 12.

41. Balz and Johnson, *The Battle for America 2008,* p. 41.

42. Institute of Politics, John F. Kennedy School of Government, *Campaign for President: The Managers Look at 2008* (Rowman and Littlefield, 2009), p. 45.

43. Balz and Johnson, *The Battle for America 2008,* pp. 21–22.

44. Dalia Sussman, "Poll Shows View of Iraq War Is Most Negative since Start," *New York Times,* July 18, 2011.

45. Balz and Johnson, *The Battle for America 2008,* pp. 21–22.

46. Anne E. Kornblut and Jon Cohen, "For Democrats, Iowa Still up for Grabs," *Washington Post,* November 20, 2001, p. A1.

47. Plouffe, *The Audacity to Win,* p. 19.

48. Ibid., pp. 19, 78, 164.

49. Nelson, "Campaigns Matter," pp. 308–09.

50. Plouffe, *The Audacity to Win,* p. 178.

51. Balz and Johnson, *The Battle for America 2008,* p. 192; see also pp. 194, 212.

52. Plouffe, *The Audacity to Win,* pp. 232, 233–34.

53. See www.realclearpolitics.com/epolls/2008/president/democratic_delegate_count.html.

54. Balz and Johnson, *The Battle for America 2008,* pp. 230, 39, 48, 28.

55. Dan Balz, "Prominent Republicans' Moves Scrutinized for Clues to 2012 Bids," *Washington Post,* June 4, 2009, p. A6; Chris Cillizza, "With Eyes on 2012 Race, Governor Launches PAC," *Washington Post,* September 23, 2009, p. A3.

56. Reid Wilson, "McCain Team Gets behind Tim Pawlenty," *The Hill,* October 13, 2009, p. 1; Reid Wilson, "House Republicans Hope to Catch up to Obama on Use of New-Media Tools," *The Hill,* October 8, 2009, p. 26; Chris Cillizza, "Pawlenty to Headline His First Iowa Event," *Washington Post,* October 8, 2009, p. A7; "Pawlenty Is First to the Starting Line in N.H.," *The Hill,* November 12, 2009, p. 10.

57. Reid Wilson, "Romney on Fundraising Tear," *The Hill,* October 6, 2009, p. 26.

58. Balz, "Prominent Republicans' Moves Scrutinized for Clues to 2012 Bids."

59. Reid Wilson, "Potential Candidates Raise Their Profiles during Invisible Primary," *The Hill,* October 6, 2009, p. 22.

Notes to Chapter 3

1. Stephen J. Wayne, *The Road to the White House 1992* (St. Martin's Press, 1992), p. 137.

2. Byron E. Shafer, *Bifurcated Politics: Evolution and Reform in the National Party Convention* (Harvard University Press, 1988), p. 257.

3. G. Terry Madonna and Michael Young, "What If the Conventions Are Contested," RealClearPolitics, December 6, 2007 (www.realclearpolitics.com/articles/2007/12/politically_uncorrected_conven.html).

4. Elizabeth Drew, *Portrait of an Election* (Simon and Schuster, 1981), p. 223.

5. Jack W. Germond and Jules Witcover, *Whose Broad Stripes and Bright Stars* (Warner Books, 1989), pp. 329, 336–50.

6. Theodore H. White, *The Making of the President 1968* (Atheneum, 1969), pp. 320, 321.

7. See Elaine C. Kamarck, *Primary Politics* (Brookings, 2009), p. 86; Ernest R. May and Janet Frazer, *Campaign 72: The Managers Speak* (Harvard University Press, 1973), p. 15.

8. Kamarck, *Primary Politics,* pp. 86–88.

9. Jack W. Germond and Jules Witcover, *Wake Us When It's Over* (Macmillan, 1985), p. 400.

10. White, *The Making of the President 1968,* pp. 319, 333.

11. Kamarck, *Primary Politics,* p. 86.

12. For a more detailed discussion of the difficulties in establishing proportional representation in the Democratic nominating process, see ibid., pp. 86–93, 118.

13. Martin Schram, *Running for President 1976: The Carter Campaign* (Stein and Day, 1977), pp. 230–31.

14. Theodore H. White, *America in Search of Itself: The Making of the President 1956–1980* (Harper and Row, 1982), pp. 329–32.

15. *National Party Conventions, 1831–1996* (Congressional Quarterly Press, 1997), p. 19.

16. *National Party Conventions, 1831–1992* (Congressional Quarterly Press, 1995), p. 119.

17. *National Party Conventions, 1831–1996*, pp. 19, 119; Gary C. Byrne and Paul Marx, *The Great American Convention: A Political History of Presidential Elections* (Pacific Book Publishing), p. 135.

18. White, *America in Search of Itself*, pp. 333, 336, 339.

19. Ibid., p. 319.

20. Germond and Whitcover, *Wake Us When It's Over*, pp. 402–03, 424.

21. Kenneth J. Garcia and Susan Yoachum, "Republican Uproar over Abortion: Pro-Choice Leaders Warn of a Convention Floor Fight," SFGate.com, August 7, 1996 (Sfgate.com/1996-08-07/news/17782026 _1_gop-platform).

22. *National Party Conventions, 1831–1996*, p. 180.

23. See www.presidency/ucsb.edu/data/vp_selection.php.

24. Germond and Witcover, *Whose Broad Stripes and Bright Stars*, p. 335.

25. Zachary Karabell, "The Rise and Fall of the Televised Political Convention," Discussion Paper D-33, Joan Shorenstein Center for Press, Politics, and Public Policy, John F. Kennedy School of Government, October 1998, pp. 3, 4, 5–6.

26. Ibid., p. 6.

27. Byron Shafer, *Bifurcated Politics* (Russell Sage, 1988), p. 261.

28. Karabell, "The Rise and Fall of the Televised Political Convention," pp. 7, 8.

29. David Folkenflik, *All Things Considered*, National Public Radio, August, 22, 2008.

30. Jonathan S. Morris and Peter L. Francia, "Losing Control? The Rise of Cable News and Its Effect on Party Convention Coverage," in *Rewiring Politics: Presidential Nominating Conventions in the Media Age*, edited by Costas Panagopoulos (Louisiana State University Press, 2007), p. 153

31. David Bauder, "Democratic Convention Ratings: 38 Million Watch Obama's Acceptance Speech," August 29, 2008 (www.huffingtonpost.com/2008/08/29/democratic-national-convention).

32. David Bauder, "Republic National Convention Ratings: John McCain Speech Ties Barack Obama's," September 5, 2008 (www.huffingtonpost.com/2008/09/05/republican-national-convention).

33. Bauder, "Democratic National Convention Ratings"; Bauder, "Republican National Convention Ratings."

NOTES TO CHAPTER 4

1. Marty Cohen and others, *The Party Decides: Presidential Nominations before and after Reform* (University of Chicago Press, 2008), p. 124.

2. Legislation has been introduced in the Nebraska legislature to return the state to a winner-take-all system, which it was before 1991. Jean Ortiz, "Bill Targets Nebraska's Ability to Split Electoral Votes" (http://journalstar.com/news/local/govt-and-politics/article_b05a487c-f).

3. Theodore H. White, *The Making of the President 1968* (Atheneum, 1969), p. 385.

4. Ibid., p. 386.

5. See www.uselectionatlas.org/RESULTS/national.php?year=1968.

6. Theodore H. White, *America in Search of Itself* (Harper and Row, 1982), pp. 380, 383.

7. This discussion is informed by a presentation by Frank Fahrenkopf to American University's Campaign Management Institute on December 31, 1991. Fahrenkopf was the chair of the Republican National Committee during the 1988 presidential election.

8. Daron R. Shaw, *The Race to 270: The Electoral College and the Campaign Strategies of 2000 and 2004* (University of Chicago Press, 2006), pp. 47, 48.

9. Ibid., p. 54; see also pp. 57, 63.

10. Ibid., pp. 58, 59, 65.

11. David Plouffe, *The Audacity to Win: The Inside Story and Lessons of Barack Obama's Historic Victory* (Viking, 2009), pp. 247–48.

12. Ibid., pp. 250, 251–52.

13. Paul Farhi, "Elephants Are Red, Donkeys Are Blue," *Washington Post,* November 2, 2004, p. C1.

14. "Illinois Senate Candidate Barack Obama, July 27, 2004, Keynote Address at the Democratic National Convention" (www.washingtonpost.com/wp-dyn/articles/A19751-2004Jul27.html).

15. Commission on Presidential Debates (www.debates.org).

16. Newton N. Minow and Craig L. LaMay, *Inside the Presidential Debates* (University of Chicago Press, 2008), p. 2. See also p. 1.

17. Joel L. Swerdlow, ed., *Presidential Debates: 1988 and Beyond* (Congressional Quarterly Press, 1987), p. ix.

18. Minow and LaMay, *Inside the Presidential Debates,* pp. 47–48.

19. Commission on Presidential Debates.

20. Minow and LaMay, *Inside the Presidential Debates,* p. 61.

21. Ibid., pp. 62–64.

22. Commission on Presidential Debates.

23. *Deadlock: The Inside Story of America's Closest Election* (Public Affairs, 2001), p. 49.

24. Ibid., p. vii; *36 Days: The Complete Chronicle of the 2000 Presidential Election Crisis* (Henry Holt, 2001), p. 8.

25. *36 Days*, p. 13.

26. *Deadlock*, p. 245.

27. Ibid., pp. 87, 135–36, 69, 79, 244; *36 Days*, p. 18.

28. *36 Days*, p. 28.

29. *Deadlock*, pp. vii, ix–xii.

30. For a detailed description of the recount process, see *Deadlock*, written by the political staff of the *Washington Post*.

31. Dan Keating and Dan Balz, "Florida Recount Would Have Favored Bush," *Washington Post*, November 30, 2001.

NOTES TO CHAPTER 5

1. National Cable and Telecommunications Association, "History of Cable Television" (www.ncta.com/About/About/HistoryofCableTelevision.aspx).

2. Darrell M. West, *The Rise and Fall of the Media Establishment* (Bedford/St. Martin's, 2001), p. 85.

3. See www.youtube.com/watch?v=D5FzCeV0ZFc.

4. Laura MacCleery, "Goodbye Soft Money, Hello Grassroots: How Campaign Finance Reform Restructured Campaigns and the Political World," *Catholic University Law Review* 58: 972.

5. Center for Public Integrity, "The Buying of the Presidency 2008" (www.buyingofthepresidency.org/index.php/archives/reports/605).

6. Garrett M. Graff, *The First Campaign: Globalization, the Web, and the Race for the White House* (Farrar, Straus and Giroux, 2007), p. 57.

7. For the following passages, see ibid., pp. 57–58, 79, 22–24, 42–44, 45.

8. Timothy D. Pollard, James W. Chesebro, and David Paul Studinski, "The Role of the Internet in Presidential Campaigns," *Communications Studies* 60, no. 5: 576.

9. Graff, *The First Campaign*, p. 49.

10. Ibid.

11. Richard Rappaport, "Net vs. Norm," May 29, 2000 (www.forbes.com/asap/2000/0529/053_print.html).

12. Judith S. Trent and Robert Friedenberg, *Political Campaign Communication: Principles and Practices*, 6th ed (Rowman and Littlefield, 2007), p. 404.

13. Graff, *The First Campaign*, pp. 65–66.

14. Michael Cornfield, "The Internet and Campaign 2004: A Look Back at the Campaigners" (www.pewinternet.org/Search.aspx?q=Michael%20Cornfield&q=%20The%20Internet%20and%20Campaign%202004%3a%20A%20Look%20Back%20at%20the%20Campaigners).

15. David B. Magleby, Anthony Corrado, and Kelly D. Patterson, eds., *Financing the 2004 Election* (Brookings, 2006), pp. 103–06.

16. See www.moveon.org/about/html.

17. Kathleen Hall Jamieson, ed., *Electing the President 2004: The Insider's View* (University of Pennsylvania Press, 2006), p. 218.

18. See www.moveon.org/pac/cands/dean/html.

19. See www.moveon.org/pac/primary/report.html.

20. Joe Trippi, *The Revolution Will Not Be Televised: Democracy, the Internet, and the Overthrow of Everything* (Harper, 2004, 2008), pp. 83, 84, 95–98.

21. Graff, *The First Campaign,* p. 71.

22. Cornfield, *"The Internet and Campaign 2004,"* p. 2.

23. See www.worldlingo.com/ma/enwiki/en/JibJab.

24. Alan Rosenblatt, "Dimensions of Campaigns in the Age of Digital Networks," in *Campaigns and Elections American Style,* edited by James A. Thurber and Candice J. Nelson, 3rd ed. (Westview, 2010), p. 215.

25. David Plouffe, *The Audacity to Win* (Viking, 2009), p. 21.

26. Aaron Smith and Lee Rainie, "The Internet and the 2008 Election," Pew Internet and American Life Project, June 15, 2008, pp. 1, 8, 4–5, 11.

27. Julie Barko Germany, "The Online Revolution," in *Campaigning for President 2008,* edited by Dennis W. Johnson (Routledge, 2009), p. 156.

28. Joshua Green, "The Amazing Money Machine" (www.theatlantic.com/magazine/archive/2008/06/the-amazing-money-machine).

29. Ibid.; Ari Melber, "Obama's Web-Savvy Voter Plan," *Nation,* October 27, 2008.

30. Melber, "Obama's Web-Savvy Voter Plan."

31. Plouffe, *The Audacity to Win,* p. 330.

32. Ibid.

33. David Usborne, "The Grandparents Being Urged to Vote Obama," *Independent,* October 11, 2008.

34. Leonard Steinhorn, "The Selling of the President in a Converged Media Age," in *Campaigns and Elections American Style,* edited by James A. Thurber and Candice J. Nelson, eds., 3rd ed. (Westview, 2009), p. 152.

35. Steinhorn, "The Selling of the President in a Converged Media Age," p. 152.

36. Tim Craig and Michael D. Shear, "Allen Quip Provokes Outrage, Apology," *Washington Post,* August 15, 2006.

37. Allen is seeking to return to public life in 2012, running for his old Senate seat. Subsequent to Allen's announcement, Webb announced that he would not seek reelection.

38. See www.time.com/time/politics/article/0,8599,1730546,00.html.

39. Plouffe, *The Audacity to Win,* p. 214.

40. Institute of Politics, John F. Kennedy School of Government, *Campaign for President: The Managers Look at 2008* (Rowman and Littlefield, 2009), p. 52.

41. Ibid., p. 50.

NOTES TO CHAPTER 6

1. A third way that African Americans were disenfranchised in the late 1880s and early 1890s was through white primaries. Southern politicians argued that the Democratic Party was a private organization, and thus party officials could decide who voted in the primaries. Because the South was dominated by the Democratic Party at the time, the primary was the major election. Excluding African Americans from the primary effectively disenfranchised them. In 1940 the U.S. Supreme Court, in *Smith* v. *Alright,* declared white primaries to be a violation of the Fifteenth Amendment and, thus, unconstitutional.

2. Alexander Keyssar, *The Right to Vote: The Contested History of Democracy in the United States* (Basic Books, 2000), pp. 277, 279–80.

3. Ibid., p. 280.

4. *Oregon* v. *Mitchell,* 400 U.S. 112 (1970).

5. Keyssar, *The Right to Vote,* p. 281.

6. Ibid., p. 275.

7. How to Register and Vote at a One-Stop Absentee Site, North Carolina Board of Elections (www.sboe.state.nc.us/content.aspx?ID=32).

8. United States Elections Project (www.elections.gmu.edu/voter_turnout.htm).

9. Barry C. Burden and others, "Election Laws, Mobilization, and Turnout: The Unanticipated Consequences of Election Reform," working paper, University of Wisconsin at Madison, 2010, p. 17.

10. Paul Gronke, Eva Galanes-Rosenbaum, and Peter A. Miller, "Early Voting and Turnout," *PS,* October 2007, p. 639.

11. National Conference of State Legislatures, "Absentee and Early Voting" (www.ncsl.org/?tabid=16604).

12. Gronke, Galanes-Rosenbaum, and Miller, "Early Voting and Turnout," p. 640.

13. National Conference of State Legislatures, "Absentee and Early Voting."

14. Robert M. Stein and Greg Vonnahme, "The Effect of Election Day Vote Centers on Voter Experience," paper prepared for the 2009 Annual Meetings of the Midwest Political Science Association, April 1–4, 2009, pp. 2, 4.

15. Priscilla L. Southwell, "Five Years Later: A Re-Assessment of Oregon's Vote by Mail Electoral Process," Department of Political Science, University of Oregon, p. 2.

16. Gronke, Galanes-Rosenbaum, and Miller, "Early Voting and Turnout," p. 642.

17. Barry C. Burden and others, "Election Laws, Mobilization, and Turnout: The Unanticipated Consequences of Election Reform," working paper, University of Wisconsin at Madison, 2010, p. 17.

18. Gronke, Galanes-Rosenbaum, and Miller, "Early Voting and Turnout"; Burden and others, "Election Laws, Mobilization, and Turnout."

19. Burden and others, "Election Laws, Mobilization, and Turnout," pp. 23, 9.

20. Gronke, Galanes-Rosenbaum, and Miller, "Early Voting and Turnout," p. 642.

21. Raymond E. Wolfinger and Steven J. Rosenstone, *Who Votes?* (Yale University Press, 1980).

22. U.S. Census Bureau, *Current Population Reports,* May 2010.

23. Frances Fox Piven and Richard A. Cloward, *Why Americans Don't Vote* (Pantheon, 1988).

24. United States Commission on Civil Rights, *The Voting Rights Act: Ten Years After* (1975), pp. 70–71.

25. Benjamin Highton, "Voter Registration and Turnout in the United States," *Perspectives on Politics* 2, no. 3 (2004): 507–15.

26. Joseph Lawler, "Motor Voter and Turnout 15 Years after the NVRA," Department of Economics, University of Notre Dame, p. 3.

27. Bob Blaemire, presentation, Campaign Management Institute, American University, May 10, 2011.

28. Wendy Weiser, "Are HAVA Provisional Ballots Working?" HAVA Conference, Center for Democracy and Election Management, American University, March 29, 2006.

29. U.S. Election Assistance Commission, "2008 Election Administration and Voting Survey," November, 2009, p. 12.

30. Ibid., pp. 14–15.

NOTES TO CHAPTER 7

1. Daniel Weiss, "Reapportionment Then and Now," *Campaigns and Elections,* February 2011, p. 13.

2. Douglas M. Johnson, "2010 Apportionment Continues 40-Year Shift to South/Southwest," report, Rose Institute of State and Local Government, December 21, 2010 (http://rosereport.org/20101221-apportionment-continues-40 -year).

3. U.S. Census (www.census.gov/population/www.socdemo/hispanic/hispanic_pop_presentation.html).

4. Chris Cillizza, "Growth in Hispanic Population Poses Challenges for Republicans," *Washington Post,* March 28, 2011, p. A2.

5. Paul R. Abramson, John H. Aldrich, and David W. Rohde, *Change and Continuity in the 2008 Elections* (Congressional Quarterly Press, 2010), p. 118.

6. See http://2010.census.gov/2010census.data.

7. Cillizza, "Growth in Hispanic Population Poses Challenges for Republicans."

8. The Current Population Survey did not measure turnout among Asians until the 1996 election.

9. These figures are turnout among eligible voters, not turnout among the entire U.S. population of each demographic group.

10. Mark Hugo Lopez and Paul Taylor, "Dissecting the 2008 Electorate: Most Diverse in U.S. History," Pew Research Center, 2009, pp. iii, 1.

11. Emily Hoban Kirby and Kei Kawashima-Ginsberg, "The Youth Vote in 2008," fact sheet, Center for Information and Research on Civic Learning and Engagement, 2009, pp. 2–4; CIRCLE, "Youth Voter Turnout up Sharply in 2004" (www.civicyouth.org/PopUps/Release_Turnout2004.pdf).

12. David Plouffe, *The Audacity to Win* (Viking, 2009), pp. 19–20.

13. Dan Balz and Haynes Johnson, *The Battle for America 2008* (Viking, 2009), pp. 106, 107.

14. Ibid., p. 105.

15. Ibid., p. 124.

16. Ibid., pp. 123, 125.

17. Plouffe, *The Audacity to Win*, p. 231.

18. Ibid., pp. 252, 256.

19. Ibid., p. 251.

20. See http://2010.census.gov/2010census/data.

21. Thomas B. Edsall and James V. Grimaldi, "On Nov. 2 GOP Got More Bang for Its Billion, Analysis Shows," *Washington Post,* December 30, 2004, p. A1.

22. Donald P. Green and Alan S. Gerber, *Get out the Vote! How to Increase Voter Turnout* (Brookings, 2004), p. 9.

23. Quoted in E. J. Dionne, "The Democrats' Rove Envy," *Washington Post,* December 14, 2004, p. A27.

24. Plouffe, *The Audacity to Win*, p. 256.

25. Balz and Johnson, *The Battle for America 2008*, p. 365.

26. Leonard Steinhorn, "The Selling of the Presidency in a Converged Media Age," in *Campaigns and Elections American Style,* edited by James A. Thurber and Candice J. Nelson, 3rd ed. (Westview, 2009), p. 151.

Notes to Chapter 8

1. "T-Paw Charts Path to the Presidency via Iowa and the Web," *Campaigns and Elections,* April 2011, p. 9.

2. Anne E. Kornblut, "Obama Picks Chicago for Reelection Headquarters," *Washington Post,* January 21, 2011, p. A5.

3. Politico, "GOP 2012 Debate Moved to Sept.," March 30, 2011 (http://dyn.politco.com/printstory.cfm?uuid=0648E4AD-9B4D-F788).

4. Part of the reason for the small field was the stringent requirements that were placed on candidates who wished to participate in the debate. Only candidates who had formed exploratory committees or announced a formal campaign, had filed the necessary paperwork with the FEC and the South Carolina state party, paid all filing fees, and averaged at least 1 percent in five national

polls were allowed to participate. Johnson announced his candidacy on April 21. Michael O'Brien, "GOP Candidates Must File with FEC to Enter First 2012 Debate," *The Hill,* April 12, 2011, p. 19.

5. Karen Tumulty, "Stage Set for First GOP Debate. So Where Are the Candidates?" *Washington Post,* May 5, 2011, p. A1.

6. "Race to the Finish," *Newsweek,* July 4/11, p. 66.

7. Chris Cillizza, "Romney Campaign Raises More than $18 Million," *Washington Post*, July 7, 2011, p. A2. The campaign raised $10.25 million in just one day in a phone-a-thon on May 16. Christina Silva, "$10 Million Day for Romney," *Washington Post,* May 17, 2011.

8. Cillizza, "Romney Campaign Raises More than $18 Million."

9. T. W. Farnam and Nia-Malika Henderson, "Huntsman Contributes to His Own Campaign," *Washington Post,* July 1, 2011, p. A4.

10. See www.opensecrets.org/pres12/summary.php.

11. Cillizza, "Romney Campaign Raises More than $18 Million."

12. Perry Bacon Jr. and Aaron Blake, "With $86 Million, Obama Sets a Fundraising Record," *Washington Post,* July 14, 2011, p. A3.

13. Philip Rucker, "Romney Loses GOP Front-Runner Status," *Washington Post,* August 25, 2011, p. A2.

14. Nicolas Confessore, "Money No Obstacle as Perry Joins G.O.P. Race," *New York Times*, August 13, 2011, p. 1.

15. Reid Wilson, "RNC Prepares to Start a Long Calendar Debate," *The Hill,* Wednesday, July 29, 2009, p. 6; Dan Balz, "There They Go Again: Fixing the Primary Process," *Washington Post,* June 28, 2009, p. A2.

16. "Republican National Committee Approves 2012 Presidential Nominating Process," August 2010, RNC news release, August 2010; *Report of the Democratic Change Commission,* December 30, 2009, p. 1.

17. Rachel Weiner, "Florida Is First Battleground for 2012 Presidential Primary Jockeying," July 5, 2011 (http://voices.washingtonpost.com/thefix/eye-on-2012/florida-first-battleground).

18. Adam C. Smith, "Florida GOP Leaders Push for Early Primary Date, Despite Threat from RNC," Politico, July 8, 2011.

19. "Republican National Committee Approves 2012 Presidential Nominating Process."

20. See www.p2012.org/chrn/oth-12.html.

21. *Report of the Democratic Change Commission,* p. 19.

22. "Democratic Party to Keep Controversial Superdelegates" (www.newsweek.com/2010/08/02/democractic-party-to-keep-controversial-delegates).

23. *Report of the Democratic Change Commission,* p. 20.

24. Mark Hugh Lopez, "Dissecting the 2008 Electorate: Most Diverse in U.S. History," Pew Research Center, April 30, 2009.

25. "Dems to Shun Corporate, PAC Money at Convention" (www.washingtonpost.com/wp-dyn/content/article/2011/02/04).

26. Aaron Smith, "22% of Online Americans Used Social Networking or Twitter for Politics in 2010 Campaign," Pew Research Center, January 27, 2011, p. 3; also see pp. 4, 7, 10.

27. Ibid., p. 11.

28. Jon Cohen and Dan Balz, "Poll: Romney Is Still GOP Front-Runner," *Washington Post,* July 21, 2011, p. A3.

29. "Obama Maintains Sub-50% Job Approval in 10th Quarter," Gallup Poll, July 21, 2011 (www.gallup.com/poll/148598/Obama-Maintains-Sub-Job-Approval-10th-Quarter.aspx?utm_source=tagrss&utm_medium=rss&utm_campaign=syndication&utm_term=Presidential Job Approval).

30. Campaign Finance Institute, "Non-Party Spending Doubled in 2010 but Did Not Dictate the Results," November 5, 2010.

31. Dan Eggen and T. W. Farnam, "Two Conservative Groups Emerge as Biggest Midterm Spenders," *Washington Post,* December 3, 2010, p. A9.

32. Dan Eggen, "Campaigning, from the Outside," *Washington Post,* July 5, 2011, p. A1.

33. Dan Eggen, "Democrats Build a Big-Money Network," *Washington Post,* April 13, 2011, p. A2; Eggen, "Campaigning, from the Outside," p. A12.

34. Eggen, "Democrats Build a Big-Money Network."

35. Dan Eggen, "Political Groups, Now Free of Limits, Spending Heavily ahead of 2012," *Washington Post,* May 22, 2011, p. A5.

36. Eggen, "Campaigning, from the Outside," p. A12.

Notes to Chapter 9

1. "Washington Suspends 2012 Primary; Regular State Primary Still On" (www.sos.wa.gov/office/osos_news.aspx?i+zwm8zI6TS07Z8O).

2. "Voter Registration and Requirements," *New York Times,* July 27, 2011.

3. Greg Allen, "Fla. GOP Pushes Controversial Voting Law Changes," National Public Radio, April 21, 2011; "Voter Registration and Requirements," *New York Times,* July 27, 2011.

4. Eric Russell, "LePage Signs Bill Banning Same-Day Voter Registration, but Critics Vow to Fight," *Bangor Daily News,* June 21, 2011.

INDEX

Page references followed by *t* refer to tables.